Collins

INTERNATIONAL PRIMARY ENGLISH

Student's Book 5

CW00569807

William Collins' dream of knowledge for all began with the publication of his first book in 1819. A self-educated mill worker, he not only enriched millions of lives, but also founded a flourishing publishing house. Today, staying true to this spirit, Collins books are packed with inspiration, innovation and practical expertise. They place you at the centre of a world of possibility and give you exactly what you need to explore it.

Collins. Freedom to teach.

Published by Collins
An imprint of HarperCollins*Publishers*
The News Building
1 London Bridge Street
London SE1 9GF

1st Floor, Watermarque Building, Ringsend Road, Dublin 4, Ireland

Browse the complete Collins catalogue at
www.collins.co.uk

ISBN 978-0-00-836767-1

British Library Cataloguing-in-Publication Data
A catalogue record for this publication is available from the British Library.

Authors: Jan Gallow and (1st edition) Fiona MacGregor
Series editor: Daphne Paizee
Publisher: Elaine Higgleton
Product developer: Natasha Paul
Project manager: Karen Williams
Development editor: Sonya Newland
Copyeditor: Karen Williams
Proofreader: Catherine Dakin
Cover designer: Gordon MacGilp
Cover illustrator: Emma Chichester Clark
Internal designer and typesetter: Ken Vail Graphic Design Ltd.
Text permissions researcher: Rachel Thorne
Image permissions researcher: Alison Prior
Illustrators: Ken Vail Graphic Design Ltd., Advocate Art, Beehive Illustration and QBS Learning
Production controller: Lyndsey Rogers
Printed and bound by Bell and Bain Ltd, Glasgow

Third-party websites, publications and resources referred to in this publication have not been endorsed by Cambridge Assessment International Education

With thanks to the following teachers and schools for reviewing materials in development: Amanda DuPratt, Shreyaa Dutta Gupta, Sharmila Majumdar, Sushmita Ray and Sukanya Singhal, Calcutta International School; Akash Raut, DSB International School, Mumbai; Melissa Brobst, International School of Budapest; Shalini Reddy, Manthan International School; Taman Rama Intercultural School.

MIX
Paper from
responsible sources
FSC™ C007454
www.fsc.org

Contents

How to use this book

Key texts and images
The texts in Stage 5 provide a wide variety of different genres for learners to enjoy. The colourful illustrations provide enjoyment as well as essential support for learners as they read. Learners will read stories by published authors and are introduced to variety of different illustration styles and images.

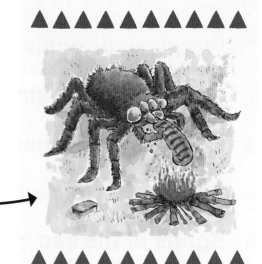

Remember boxes
These are used to remind learners to do things that they have already learned, such as the correct use of punctuation marks.

Remember!
Choose words that express your viewpoint and which create feeling and mood.

Spelling log
These are used throughout this course. Spelling logs allow learners to compile their own personal dictionaries which they can refer to in their writing activities. They also help learners to develop dictionary skills.

Spelling log
Write any new words in your spelling log.

Thinking time
These occur at the end of each unit in the Student's Book. Learners are encouraged to reflect on what they have read, listened to, discussed and learned.

Thinking time
Which folk tales and fairy tales have you read? Which is your most and least favourite? Why?

1 What's your name?

Listening and speaking

1 Listen as your teacher reads you the first pages of a book called *Saffy's Angel*. The story begins with a flashback to the day Saffron learns something that changes her life.

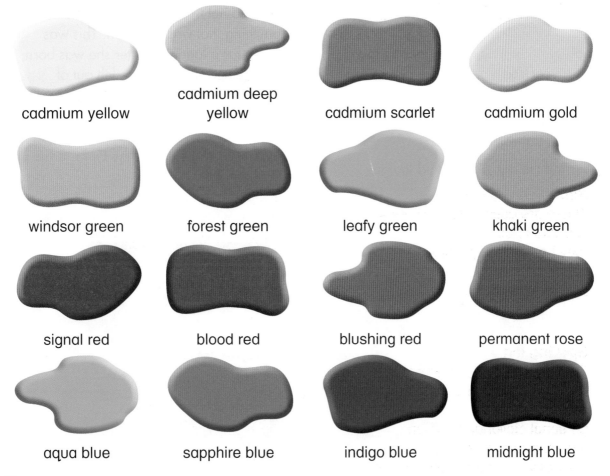

cadmium yellow	cadmium deep yellow	cadmium scarlet	cadmium gold
windsor green	forest green	leafy green	khaki green
signal red	blood red	blushing red	permanent rose
aqua blue	sapphire blue	indigo blue	midnight blue

2 **GROUP WORK. Talk about the questions below. Think carefully about what you heard and give reasons for your responses.**

a How did the Casson children get their names?

b How many colours did you hear? Make a list.

c What lullabies did you have as a child? What did the Casson children have instead?

d Why did Indigo's name suit him?

e What problem does Saffron have?

1

Reading and vocabulary

PAIR WORK. Read the next page of *Saffy's Angel*. Look out for names and colour words as you read.

Realistic fiction

Fiction means 'not true', but realistic fiction refers to stories that could be true. They:

- resemble real life.
- have a believable setting.
- include events that could happen and issues that are resolved in realistic ways.

Indigo was crouched on the hearth rug sorting through the coal bucket. Pieces of coal lay all around. Sometimes he found lumps speckled with what he believed to be gold.

"Come and help me look for Saffron!" pleaded Saffron.

"Find the baby first," said Indigo.

Indigo did not like the baby to be left out of anything that was going on. This was because for a long time after she was born, it had seemed she would be left out of everything, for ever. She had very nearly eluded his pack. She had very nearly died. Now she was safe and easy to find, third row up at the end of the Pinks. Rose. Permanent Rose.

Rose was screaming because the health visitor had arrived to look at her. She had turned up unexpectedly from beyond the black, rainy windows, and picked up Rose with her strong, cold hands, and so Rose was screaming.

"Make Rose shut up!" shouted Saffron from her stool. "I'm trying to read!"

"Saffron reads anything now!" the children's mother told the health visitor, proudly.

"Very nice!" the health visitor replied, and Saffron looked pleased for a moment, but then stopped when the health visitor added that her twins had both been fluent readers at four years old, and had gone right through their junior school library by the age of six.

Saffron glanced across to Caddy, the eldest of the Casson children, to see if this could possibly be true. Caddy, aged thirteen, was absorbed in painting the soles of her hamster's feet, but she felt Saffron's unhappiness and gave her a quick comforting smile.

Since Rose's arrival the Casson family had heard an awful lot about the health visitor's multi-talented twins. They were in Caddy's class at school. There were a number of rude and true things Caddy might have said about them, but being Caddy, she kept them to herself. Her smile was enough.

Caddy appeared over and over on the colour chart, all along the top row.

Cadmium lemon, Cadmium deep yellow, Cadmium scarlet and Cadmium gold.

No Saffron though.

"There isn't a Saffron," said Saffron after another long search. "I've looked, and there isn't! I've read it all, and there *isn't!*"

Nobody seemed to hear at first.

Indigo said, "Saffron's yellow."

"I *know* Saffron's yellow! I've looked under *all* the yellows," said Saffron loudly and belligerently, "and I've looked under *all* the oranges too, and there *isn't* a Saffron!"

Rose wailed louder, because she didn't want to be undressed. Her mother said, "Oh darling! Darling!" Indigo began hammering at likely-looking lumps of coal with the handle end of the poker. Caddy let the hamster walk across the table, and it made a delicate and beautiful pattern of rainbow-coloured footprints all over the health visitor's notes.

"Why isn't there a Saffron?" demanded Saffron. "There's all the others. What about me?"

Then the health visitor said the thing that changed Saffron's life. She looked up from unpicking something out of Rose's clenched fist, and said to the children's mother:

"Doesn't Saffron know?"

Comprehension

1 **Say if the sentences below are true or false. Correct the false ones so they fit the story.**

a Indigo found lumps of gold in coal.

b Rose, who is the baby, almost died.

c Saffron was calmly reading the chart.

d Saffron reads better than the health visitor's children.

e Cadmium's name appears five times on the colour chart.

f Saffron is a golden yellow colour.

g Rose wailed because she was cold.

h The health visitor was trying to make Rose smile.

2 **PAIR WORK. Talk about the questions below. Then write the answers.**

a Why do you think the family call the baby Permanent Rose?

b What does Saffron think about the health visitor and her children?

c Find a phrase that tells us the health visitor thinks her children are better than the Casson children.

d What would Caddy say about the health visitor's children if she could?

e What do you think Saffron doesn't know?

Remember!

To complete Activity 1, you only need to look at the explicit or literal meaning of the text.

To complete Activity 2, you need to consider implicit meaning. This means that you need to infer or read between the lines about what the writer means.

Using nouns

Nouns

Nouns are the names of people, places and things.

- **Common nouns** are the names of everyday, ordinary things, for example: desk, chair, brother.

- **Proper nouns** are the names of people or places – they start with a capital letter, for example: Saffron, Indigo, London, Brown Street.

- **Abstract nouns** name something that you can't touch, like loyalty, love or impatience.

Most nouns can be counted. **Countable nouns** can be singular (one) or plural (many), for example: hamster / hamsters.

Some nouns cannot be counted. **Uncountable nouns** are usually singular. They do not have plurals, for example: milk, homework.

1 Look at the text again. Find examples of: proper nouns, uncountable nouns, countable nouns and abstract nouns.

2 Choose the correct word to complete the sentences.

a Why has my colour chart got fewer/less colours on it?

b Pass me the bucket with fewer/less coal.

c Saffron read fewer/less books than the twins.

d She should spend fewer/less time watching television and more time reading.

e My sandpit has fewer/less sand than yours.

Remember!

Use *fewer* with countable nouns.

Use *less* with uncountable nouns.

Thinking deeper

- What part of speech do you think colours are? What words do they tell you more about?
- Write a list of all the colour words you know. Who in the class has the longest list?

Spelling and vocabulary

Plurals

When you make a noun plural, you usually just add an *–s*. But:

- if the word ends in a consonant + *y*, drop the *y* and add *–ies*
- if the word ends in *ch*, *sh*, *s*, *ss* or *x*, add *–es*.

For example: lullab**y** lullab**ies**

baby bab**ies**

bo**x** box**es**

lun**ch** lunch**es**

Exceptions to the rules

Some nouns stay the same, for example:
bread, buck, fish, series, moose.

Some nouns change their spelling, for example: foot   foot,
man – men, woman – women, ox – oxen.

Some nouns are always plural, for example:
pants, pyjamas, clothes, cattle, news.

1 **Change the nouns in brackets into the plural form.**

In the (holiday), we took our (lunch) to the public (garden) and sat on the wooden (bench) to eat and watch the people. We heard (baby) crying, (child) playing and (taxi) hooting. We checked our (watch) after lunch and it was time to go home.

2 **Correct the mistakes in the sentences below.**

a Caddy told her sister storys about fairys.

b They washed the dishs and then dried them with clothes.

c She used different coloures to paint the womans.

d There are potatos on the shelfs.

e The radioes were blaring, so I couldn't hear the announcementes.

3 **PAIR WORK. What consonant pattern is in each word below?**

through   eight   enough   thought   weight
tough   though

Spelling log

Write any new words in your spelling log.

a Say the words out loud. What sound does the consonant pattern make?

b Make a sentence with each word.

c Learn the words for a spelling test.

Reading

PAIR WORK. Read the information about paragraphs. Then read the text on page 7 together. As you read:

- find the topic sentences.
- find the supporting sentences.

Paragraphs

A paragraph has:

- a topic sentence which gives the main idea of the paragraph – this is usually the first sentence
- two or three supporting sentences that expand on the topic sentence
- a concluding sentence if it is the last paragraph, or a linking sentence if it links to the next paragraph.

I should explain right off that my real name is Salamanca Tree Hiddle. Salamanca, my parents thought, was the name of the Indian tribe to which my great-great grandmother belonged. My parents were mistaken. The name of the tribe was Seneca, but since my parents did not discover their error until after I was born, and they were, by then, used to my name, it remained Salamanca.

My middle name, Tree, comes from your basic tree, a thing of such beauty to my mother that she made it part of my name.

She wanted to be more specific and use Sugar Maple Tree, her very favourite, because Sugar Maple is part of her own name, But Salamanca Sugar Maple Tree Hiddle sounded a bit much.

My mother called me Salamanca, but after she left, only my grandparents Hiddle called me Salamanca (when they were not calling me Chickabiddy). To most other people, I was Sal, and to a few boys who thought they were especially amusing, I was Salamander.

Comprehension

Answer the questions below.

a Who is the narrator in this text?

b What is funny about the way she was named?

c Why is her middle name 'Tree'?

d List the names of the people in the text, and then next to their names, write down what each person called Salamanca.

e What kind of word is 'chickabiddy'?

f Where does the name 'Sal' come from?

g Would you like to be called 'Salamander'? Say why, or why not.

h How do you think she feels about her name?

i Find an abstract noun in the text.

Reading, speaking and writing

1 **Research what your own name means. Speak to your parents and look up your name on the internet or in a book in the library. Make notes about the points below.**

- the place your name comes from
- the language it comes from
- its meaning
- how you feel about your name

2 **Use your notes to help you write paragraphs about your name. Write out your paragraphs neatly or type them. Check your work using the evaluation checklist on the next page. Help your partner to check their work too.**

Writing checklist

Spelling

Is all of your spelling correct?

Have you used the internet or a dictionary to check the spelling and meaning of difficult words?

Punctuation

Have you used full stops at the end of sentences?

Have you started each sentence with a capital letter?

Grammar

Are your sentences properly constructed?

Are your tenses correct?

Do subjects agree with verbs in tense and number?

Paragraphs

Do your paragraphs have a topic sentence?

Are there supporting sentences?

Does the content inform?

Does the content make sense?

Reading and speaking

**GROUP WORK. Read the information on the next page about names.
Then read the questions below carefully and talk about the answers.**

a   Which piece of information is the most interesting? Why do you think this?

b   What is the purpose of each piece of text?

c   Who would want to read the information?

d   Share any other naming traditions you may know with your group.

e   Which key features are used in the texts?

f   How does the language differ in the texts?

g   In which piece of information is the meaning the:
   • most clear?   • least clear?

h   How are the texts different to other texts in Unit 1?

GROUP WORK RULES

Give everyone a turn to speak
Respect others and their ideas
Offer your ideas and opinions
Use soft voices
Participate
Stay focused

Chinese given names

If you are introduced to a Chinese person whose name, say, is **Liu Dai Lin**, then **Liu** is the family name, or surname. The name in the middle is a generation name, shared by all the children, or by all the children of the same gender, of a particular couple. The generation name, plus the third name in the group, becomes the child's personal name – **Dai Lin**.

Most musical names

A music-loving family in Honolulu named their children Dodo, Rere, Mimi, Fafa, Soso, Lala, Sisi and Octavia. These 'names' are from a famous 1964 musical film called 'The Sound of Music'.

Origin of some names

Alexander	historical; Greek; 'defending men'
Alice	literary; Old German; 'nobility'
Angharad	Welsh; 'loved one'
Bashir	Arabic; 'bringer of good news'
Bridget	historical; 'the high one'
Diana	mythological; name of the moon goddess
Edwin	royal; Old English; 'happy friend'
Farah	Arabic; 'joy, cheerfulness'
Junku	Japanese; 'purity'
Kwaku	West African; 'Wednesday's child, born on Wednesday'

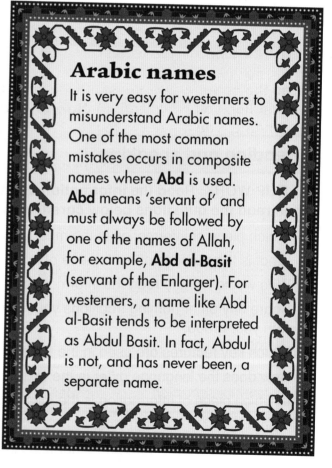

Arabic names

It is very easy for westerners to misunderstand Arabic names. One of the most common mistakes occurs in composite names where **Abd** is used. **Abd** means 'servant of' and must always be followed by one of the names of Allah, for example, **Abd al-Basit** (servant of the Enlarger). For westerners, a name like Abd al-Basit tends to be interpreted as Abdul Basit. In fact, Abdul is not, and has never been, a separate name.

Answer the questions below.

a If your Chinese name is Wu Ying Ha, what is your surname and what is your first name?

b What does 'a generation name' mean?

c What does 'Abd' mean in Arabic?

d Find two other Arabic names and write down what they mean.

e Where does the name 'Alexander' come from?

f Find a name that means 'happy friend'.

g If you wanted to name a child born on a Wednesday, what would you name them?

h Which two names have similar meanings?

i Say which name in the list you like best and why.

j Write down what you think 'Octavia' means.

Speaking

Read the notes you made in activity 2 on page 8. Add any new information you have learned. Now prepare a short talk about your name. You are going to give this talk to your class.

Giving a short talk

- Take a deep breath before you start to help you feel calm.
- You can use your notes, but look up and make eye contact with your audience after each main point.
- Speak clearly and precisely.
- Use gestures and movement to make the presentation more interesting.
- Thank the audience when you finish.

Collective nouns

A **collective noun** is the name for a group of objects, people or creatures.

For example: a **bunch** of bananas
a **flock** of birds

Or, as Indigo says in the text, a **pack** of sisters.

1 Complete the collective nouns below. Choose words from the box.

swarm suit school constellation circle suite
convoy series shush mall

a   a _____ of fish

b   a _____ of events

c   a _____ of stars

d   a _____ of shops

e   a_____ of friends

f   a _____ of trucks

g   a _____ of flies

h   a _____ of clothes

i   a _____ of furniture

j   a _____ of librarians

2 Find 15 new words from Unit 1 in the word search. List them alphabetically.

c	o	l	o	u	r	k	n	i	p
a	b	u	c	d	e	f	g	h	e
i	j	l	o	u	d	k	l	m	r
l	n	l	o	r	e	h	t	o	m
i	p	a	n	x	i	o	u	s	a
b	q	b	a	r	s	t	u	v	n
r	h	y	m	e	e	d	u	l	e
a	w	x	e	s	n	i	w	t	n
r	y	z	a	b	e	b	i	r	t
y	e	l	l	o	w	c	d	e	f

Reading and writing

1 Writers show a viewpoint through a character's opinions about a setting and other characters. Read the texts below from *Saffy's Angel*.

> She had turned up unexpectedly from beyond the **black**, **rainy** windows, and picked up Rose with her **strong**, **cold** hands, and so Rose was screaming.

> Since Rose's arrival the Casson family had heard **an awful lot** about the health visitor's multi-talented twins.

a What do the bold words tell you about Saffy's opinion of the health visitor?

b If 'an awful lot' was replaced with 'incredible tales', how would it change the meaning of the sentence?

c How does the writer's choice of words convey feeling and mood?

2 Imagine you are like Saffron in *Saffy's Angel* – someone says something that changes your life. Write four paragraphs about how you might feel and what might happen.

Copy the spider diagram below. Add key words to your diagram as you plan.

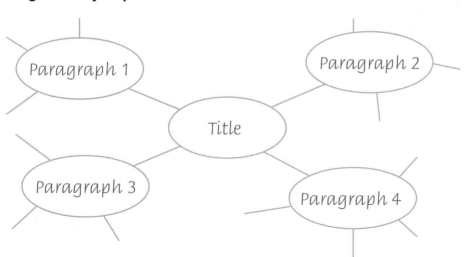

Paragraph 1
Paragraph 2
Title
Paragraph 3
Paragraph 4

3 Use the detailed story planning frame that your teacher will give you to guide you in the writing process.

Remember!

Choose words that express your viewpoint and which create feeling and mood.

GROUP WORK. Listen to the text below from the poem *The Song of Hiawatha Part 3: Hiawatha's Childhood.* As you listen, take note of the rhythm. Practise reading it aloud and then read it to the class.

Then the little Hiawatha
Learned of every bird its language,
Learned their names and all their secrets,
How they built their nests in Summer,
Where they hid themselves in Winter,
Talked with them whene'er he met them,
Called them "Hiawatha's Chickens."

Of all beasts he learned the language,
Learned their names and all their secrets,
How the beavers built their lodges,
Where the squirrels hid their acorns,
How the reindeer ran so swiftly,
Why the rabbit was so timid,
Talked with them whene'er he met them,
Called them "Hiawatha's Brothers".

Then Iagoo, the great boaster,
He the marvellous story-teller,
He the traveller and the talker,
He the friend of old Nokomis,
Made a bow for Hiawatha;
From a branch of ash he made it,
From an oak-bough made the arrows,
Tipped with flint, and winged with feathers,
And the cord he made of deer-skin.

Then he said to Hiawatha:
"Go, my son, into the forest,
Where the red deer herd together,
Kill for us a famous roebuck,
Kill for us a deer with antlers!"

Forth into the forest straightway
All alone walked Hiawatha
Proudly, with his bow and arrows;
And the birds sang round him, o'er him,
"Do not shoot us, Hiawatha!"
Sang the robin, the Opechee,
Sang the bluebird, the Owaissa,
"Do not shoot us, Hiawatha!"

Thinking time

Which text did you enjoy reading the most in Unit 1? Why?

2 Strange school stories

1 **Look at the pictures. Match the words in the box to the pictures.**

> billboard   flyer   brochure
> classified advertisement

A

Fly to Greece and bring a friend along for free.
Sun, sand and sea for only 99 dollars return.
Offer ends 2 August.
Apply now, today. Call 0800 1234

B

Speed kills. Buckle up.

C **10% off**
your **Parlour pizza**
if you bring this
flyer with you!!!
14 Shoreditch Road,
Somerset.
This offer includes
a free coke. Don't
delay, come and
dine today.

D

Bike for sale. Almost new.
Black frame and basket.
20 dollars ono.
Call 076 000 435

2 **Now talk about each kind of writing.**

a Where would you find text like this?

b What is the purpose of each kind of text?

c What is the same about them?

d What is different?

e What kind of language does each text use?

f What is the purpose of this kind of language?

Persuasive texts

Persuasive texts are used to persuade you to:

- buy something.
- do something.
- believe something.

They use adjectives and adverbs to try to convince you, for example:

Buy this *shiny new* car!

Vote *now* to save the *endangered* rhinoceros.

15

1 Skim the brochures for two different schools. As you skim:

   a notice what each brochure looks like.

   b look for similarities and differences between the schools.

2 GROUP WORK. Talk about the two brochures.

   a What kind of school is each?

   b In what ways do the two brochures look the same?

   c What is different about the information in each brochure?

   d Give **two** reasons why you would not like to go to one of the schools.

   e Do you think your parents would choose the same school as you chose? Give **one** reason for your answer.

   f What do you imagine the teachers would be like in each school? Would they be similar or different to each other?

   g In which school do you think sport has a higher profile?

3 Read the persuasive brochures. Find facts and opinions.

> **Remember!**
> We **skim** a text to gain a general idea of the contents.

1

embracing the development of the whole child

2

RODHAM ACADEMY

Excellence is all; excellence in all.

Fact or opinion?

A **fact** is information that can be proved to be true.
Mr Trumble is the headmaster of Rodham Academy.

An **opinion** is a personal view that may or may not be true.
I think Mr Trumble is an excellent headmaster.

Group work is an important part of complete child development.

Each child is nurtured and encouraged to develop their special skills at their own pace.

Exercise and taking part in team sports builds healthy bodies, and develops a sense of community spirit among the class.

Crawford College produces successful, confident citizens who can interact in all areas of society.

At Crawford College:
- classes are small
- individual tuition is available
- parent involvement in the learning process is encouraged
- scholarships are offered for those in need.

For further details, and to book an appointment, please contact MsAshcroft@emailaddress.

Our spacious grounds and excellent facilities encourage all sportspeople to reach their full potential.

Academic excellence is prized and encouraged with a rigorous programme of after-school tuition.

Our staff are all graduates of respected universities, and we cater for children who wish to study further.

Computer lab work is an important part of our career-focused curriculum.

For more information, please write to the headmaster, Mr Trumble, at:
Rodham Academy
Bainbridge Way
West Village
WE5 SJ10
Alternatively, you can contact the school secretary, MissBrown@ emailaddress.
Please include a reference from your child's previous school, as well as their latest report, with your enquiry.

Comprehension

1 Scan the brochures again. Find the persuasive features in the brochures.

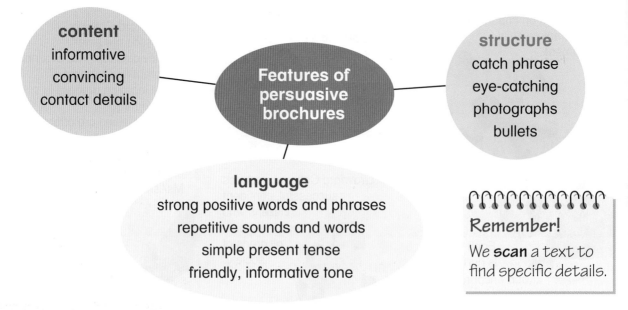

content
informative
convincing
contact details

Features of persuasive brochures

structure
catch phrase
eye-catching
photographs
bullets

language
strong positive words and phrases
repetitive sounds and words
simple present tense
friendly, informative tone

Remember!
We **scan** a text to find specific details.

2 Now read the brochures. Then answer the questions below.

Brochure 1

a Find another word for 'whole'.

b Which persuasive features have been used on the front page (see page 16)? What consonants are repeated in the name of the school?

c Find two words that mean 'helping'.

d If you look at the pictures, along with the words, what is the main focus of the school?

e What kind of person would do best at Crawford College?

Brochure 2

a Find three adjectives in the caption for the first photograph inside.

b Which word is repeated three times in the brochure? What effect does this have?

c Why do you think the brochure uses words like 'graduates' and 'respected'?

d If you look at the pictures, along with the words, what do you think is the main focus of the school?

e What kind of person would do best at Rodham Academy?

3 Create a spider diagram to make notes about one of the schools. Use the subheadings: 'Academics', 'Sport', 'Teachers', 'Other'.

Using adjectives

1 **Match each adjective to its meaning.**

1	complete	**a**	well-known and important
2	special	**b**	has done well in life
3	healthy	**c**	in good physical condition
4	successful	**d**	firm and not to be changed
5	spacious	**e**	whole
6	excellent	**f**	better than others like it
7	rigorous	**g**	unique
8	respected	**h**	big and open

2 **Now use each adjective in a sentence to show you understand its meaning.**

3 **Play the opposite game. Change the words in bold to words that mean the opposite.**

Our **excellent** school has **huge** fields and **beautiful** buildings. It is a **new** school, and is equipped with **modern** facilities. The teachers are all very **intelligent** and they **love** children, and are **happy** to help them. The atmosphere is **relaxed** and, because of this, we achieve **fantastic** results.

Spelling log

Record interesting adjectives from the brochures in your spelling log.

Writing

Imagine you are at one of the schools in the brochure. Write and tell your family two interesting pieces of information about the school.

19

Listening and writing

1 Listen as your teacher reads you the introduction to a book called *Sideways Stories from Wayside School*.

2 Draw a picture of the school.
Label:

- the school building.
- the storeys.
- the playground.

3 What is the difference between a storey and a story?

> ### Humorous fiction
> Humorous stories:
> - are designed to entertain and amuse.
> - include characters who act in a unique way.
> - may include surprising events.

Listening and reading

Now listen to the first story from *Sideways Stories from Wayside School*.

A Package for Mrs Jewls

Louis, the yard teacher, frowned.

The school yard was a mess. There were pencils and pieces of paper everywhere. How'd all this junk get here? he wondered. Well, I'm not going to pick it up!

It wasn't his job to pick up garbage. He was just supposed to pass out the balls during lunch and recess, and also make sure the kids didn't kill each other.

He sighed, then began cleaning it up. He loved all the children at Wayside School. He didn't want them playing on a dirty playground.

As he was picking up the pencils and pieces of paper, a large truck drove into the parking lot. It honked its horn twice, then twice more.

Louis ran to the truck. "Quiet!" he whispered. "Children are trying to learn in there!" He pointed at the school.

A short man with big, bushy hair stepped out of the truck. "I have a package for somebody named Mrs Jewls," he said.

"I'll take it," said Louis.

"Are you Mrs Jewls?" asked the man.

"No," said Louis.

"I have to give it to Mrs Jewls," said the man.

Louis thought for a moment. He didn't want the man disturbing the children. He knew how much they hated to be interrupted when they were working.

"I'm Mrs Jewls," he said.

"But you just said you weren't Mrs Jewls," said the man.

"I changed my mind," said Louis.

The man got the package out of the back of the truck and gave it to Louis. "Here you go, Mrs Jewls," he said.

"Uhh!" Louis grunted. It was a very heavy package. The word FRAGILE was printed on every side. He had to be careful not to drop it.

The package was so big, Louis couldn't see where he was going. Fortunately he knew the way to Mrs Jewls's class by heart. It was straight up.

Wayside School was thirty storeys high, with only one room on each storey. Mrs Jewls's class was at the very top. It was Louis's favourite class.

He pushed through the door to the school, then started up the stairs. There was no elevator.

There were stairs that led down to the basement, too, but nobody ever went down there. There were dead rats living in the basement.

The box was pressed against Louis's face, squashing his nose. Even so, when he reached the fifteenth floor, he could smell Miss Mush cooking in the cafeteria. It smelled like she was making mushrooms. Maybe on my way back I'll stop by Miss Mush's room and get some mushrooms, he thought. He didn't want to miss Miss Mush's mushrooms. They were her speciality.

He huffed and groaned and continued up the stairs. His arms and legs were very sore, but he didn't want to rest. This package might be important, he thought. I have to get it to Mrs Jewls right away.

He stepped easily from the eighteenth storey to the twentieth. There was no nineteenth storey.

Miss Zarves taught the class on the nineteenth storey. There was no Miss Zarves.

At last he struggled up the final step to the thirtieth storey. He knocked on Mrs Jewls's door with his head.

Mrs Jewls was in the middle of teaching her class about gravity when she heard the knock. "Come in," she called.

"I can't open the door," Louis gasped. "My hands are full. I have a package for you."

Mrs Jewls faced the class. "Who wants to open the door for Louis?" she asked.

All the children raised their hands. They loved to be interrupted when they were working.

"Oh dear, how shall I choose?" asked Mrs Jewls. "I have to be fair about this. I know! We'll have a spelling bee. And the winner will get to open the door.

Louis knocked his head against the door again. "It's heavy," he complained. "And I'm very tired."

"Just a second," Mrs Jewls called back. "Allison, the first word's for you. Heavy."

"Heavy," said Allison. "H-E-A-V-Y. Heavy."

"Very good. Jason, you're next. Tired."

"Tired," said Jason. "S-L-E-E-P-Y. Tired."

Louis felt the package slipping from his sweaty fingers. He shifted his weight to get a better grip. The corners of the box dug into the sides of his arms. He felt his hands go numb.

Actually, he didn't feel them go numb. "Jenny, package."

"Package," said Jenny. "B-O-X. Package."

"Excellent!" said Mrs Jewls.

Louis felt like he was going to faint.

At last John opened the door. "I won the spelling bee, Louis!" he said.

"Very good, John," muttered Louis.

"Aren't you going to shake my hand?" asked John.

Louis shifted the box to one arm, quickly shook John's hand, then grabbed the box again and staggered into the room.

"Where do you want it, Mrs Jewls?" he asked.

"I don't know," said Mrs Jewls. "What is it?"

"I don't know," said Louis. "I'll have to put it down someplace so you can open it."

"But how can I tell you where to put it until I know what it is?" asked Mrs Jewls. "You might put it in the wrong place."

So Louis held the box as Mrs Jewls stood on a chair next to him and tore open the top. His legs wobbled beneath him.

"It's a computer!" exclaimed Mrs Jewls. Everybody booed.

"What's the matter?" asked Louis. "I thought everyone loved computers."

"We don't want it, Louis." said Eric Bacon.

"Take it back, Jack," said Terrence.

"Get that piece of junk out of here," said Maurecia.

"Now, don't be that way," said Mrs Jewls. "The computer will help us learn. It's a lot quicker than a pencil and paper."

"But the quicker we learn, the more work we have to do," complained Todd.

"You may set it over there on the counter, Louis." said Mrs Jewls.

Louis set the computer on the counter next to Sharie's desk. Then he collapsed on the floor.

"Now watch closely," said Mrs Jewls.

Everyone gathered around the new computer. It had a full-colour monitor and two disc drives.

Mrs Jewls pushed it out the window.

They all watched it fall and smash against the sidewalk.

"See?" said Mrs Jewls. "That's gravity."

"Oh, now I get it!" said Joe.

"Thank you Louis," said Mrs Jewls. "I've been trying to teach them about gravity all morning. We've been using pencils and paper, but the computer was a lot quicker."

Speaking

1 GROUP WORK. Talk about the questions below.

a Did you like the story? Why or why not?

b What surprising events happened in the story?

c Did the teachers behave in the way you expect teachers to behave? Give reasons for your answer.

d Did any parts of the story make you laugh? Describe these parts to your group.

2 The writer, Louis Sachar, is American. Some American words are different from Standard English words. Match the words in the two columns.

1	yard	a	lorry
2	garbage	b	lift
3	recess	c	breaktime
4	horn	d	grounds
5	elevator	e	hooter
6	truck	f	rubbish

Comprehension

Read the story again on your own. Then answer the questions below.

a Why were there bits of paper and pencils lying in the yard?

b What was Louis's job?

c Why did the delivery man give the package to Louis?

d Where was Mrs Jewls's classroom?

e What did Louis want to do on the way back down the stairs?

f Who was Miss Zarves?

g How did Mrs Jewls choose someone to open the door?

h How do you think Louis felt while he waited?

i Why did Todd not want a computer in the classroom?

j How did Mrs Jewls finally teach the children about gravity?

Make a brochure advertising Wayside School. Be creative!
Use the chart below to guide you in the writing process.

Step 1: Planning

Think about the following things and make some notes.

Purpose
- What is the purpose of your brochure?

Front cover
- What information will go on the front?
- Which bold graphics will you include?
- What is your tagline (catchphrase or slogan) going to be?
- How will you make it eye-catching?

Inside
- What information is needed?
- What are your headings?
- What pictures and captions will you include?
- How will you use the limited space wisely?

Back cover
- What information is needed?
- What are your headings?
- How will you tell the readers what you want them to do?
- Which contact details will you include?

Step 2: Making a rough draft

Use your notes to help you write a rough draft of your brochure.
- Consider the purpose.
- Use persuasive words.
- Use headings.
- Write short sentences.
- Write lists instead of long paragraphs.
- Describe how the features will help the reader.
- Construct sentences properly.
- Use punctuation correctly.
- Include empty frames for pictures.

Step 3: Evaluate and present

Read your rough draft out loud to yourself and make corrections.

Show your brochure to your partner. Can they give suggestions to make it more persuasive?

Decide on an appropriate way to layout and present the brochure.

Decide which writing implements you will use if you are doing the brochure by hand.

Make a final version of your brochure, including all of the changes.

Vary your handwriting or font styles for headings, information and captions.

1 **Read the persuasive commentary on the right.**

Rhetorical question – questions that do not expect an answer. They encourage the reader to think about your point of view.

Exaggeration is an over-the-top statement that makes a situation seem worse than it is.

Repetition

Connectives put ideas in order and link paragraphs.

alliteration

Emotive language (strong adjectives and adverbs) makes the reader feel different emotions

RIDICULOUS NO-HOMEWORK POLICY!

Wayside School recently introduced a no-homework policy. **Have you ever heard of such a ridiculous idea?** Just thinking about it makes me want to explode! I **really** believe that students **really** benefit from doing homework.

Firstly, there is not enough time in class to reinforce the content of lessons. Students need extra practice so they can fully understand the concepts taught in class. If they do not practise the concepts, they may forget them. If they forget work they have done in class, they will do disastrously in tests and exams.

Secondly, homework trains students to be disciplined and responsible. Being disciplined and doing homework responsibly each night prepares students for the rigours of the working world.

Thirdly, homework encourages good time management. Homework has a deadline and life is full of deadlines. Students are learning skills that will help them later on in life.

Finally, a lack of homework contributes to a lack of control over students. To illustrate my point, after Wayside school abandoned homework there was an increase in vandalism and disrespectful behaviour. The school buildings were defaced with **g**ross **g**raffiti and an old man was knocked over by students skateboarding **menacingly** through a mall. As far as I am concerned, the young people responsible for these incidents should be at home doing homework, not roaming around aimlessly.

Wayside School needs to rethink their 'no-homework' policy right now!

2 **Talk about the questions below.**

a What is the text's purpose?

b Who do you think wrote it?

c Which audience do you think it is written for?

d Which features are used to persuade the listener?

e How is the commentary different to the brochures?

f How is the commentary similar to the brochures?

3 **Plan and present a commentary to persuade the leaders of your school that homework should be abolished.**

4 **PAIR WORK. Listen to your partner's commentary and give them feedback about it.**

● What went well?

● What could be improved next time?

● Was it persuasive? Give reasons to support your answer.

Thinking deeper

What is odd about the text below, and how would you correct it?

Louis held the box in Louis's arms. Louis was tired. Louis had to give the box to Mrs Jewls. Mrs Jewls was on the 30th storey. The 30th storey was a long climb. Louis couldn't wait to hand the box to Mrs Jewls.

1 **Choose the correct personal pronoun.**

a Mrs Jewls was walking up the stairs when she met (they/them).

b (We/Us) are learning about gravity.

c (She/He) put on his shoes, and then (he/she) left.

d Don't make (he/him) angry.

e The cows that are mooing belong to (their/them).

f Please let (me/us) help, (I/me) am good at Maths.

g (They/We) felt proud of (our/their) school – it was theirs.

h (You/It) look like (you/your) need help!

i (She/Her) lessons are always interesting. (She/Her) prepares well.

j The box was pushed against (his/him) face. (He/His) was struggling to see past (him/it).

k (We/Us) are grateful that Louis helped (we/us).

l (Them/They) loved to be interrupted while (them/they) were learning.

Personal pronouns

Personal pronouns are used in the place of nouns.

Subject pronouns replace the subject of the sentence. Object pronouns replace the object of the sentence.

For example:
Louis gave the box to **Mrs Jewls**.
He gave the box to **her**.

Subject pronouns	Object pronouns
I	me
he	him
she	her
it	it
we	us
you	you
they	them

2 Replace the nouns in bold below with personal pronouns.

Mrs Jewls was teaching the class about mammals. "All mammals have hair," **Mrs Jewls** said.

Bebe raised her hand. "Is my father a mammal?" **Bebe** asked.

"Yes, all people are mammals," Mrs Jewls said.

"But **my father** doesn't have any hair," said Bebe. "**My father** is bald!"

The children all laughed.

Possessive pronouns

Possessive pronouns replace the noun and show ownership. Mine, his, hers, yours, ours and theirs are possessive pronouns.

For example: The book is <u>mine</u>; the dog is <u>hers</u>.

3 Look at the chart below and write the new sentences using the correct possessive pronouns.

I have a computer.	It is my computer.	The computer is mine.
_____ has a scooter.	It is his scooter.	The scooter is _____.
_____ has a new bike.	It is her bike.	The bike is _____.
_____ have a house.	It is our house.	The house is _____.
_____ have good shoes.	They are your shoes.	The shoes are _____.
_____ have a kitten.	It is their kitten.	The kitten is _____.

4 Write a paragraph in which you use at least four personal pronouns and four possessive pronouns.

Speaking and listening

GROUP WORK.

1 Read the poem on the next page aloud.

2 Present the poem to the class.

- Decide who will say which lines, or if you will all read in chorus.
- Decide which non-verbal techniques you will use. Are you going to act out what happens? Will you wear costumes?
- Practise until you can read the lines smoothly, or see if you can learn the poem by heart.

Remember!

Show your ideas and meaning through your speech, gestures and movements.

Falling asleep in class

I fell asleep in class today,
as I was awfully bored.
I laid my head upon my desk
and closed my eyes and snored.

I woke to find a piece of paper
sticking to my face.
I'd slobbered on my textbooks,
and my hair was a disgrace.

My clothes were badly rumpled,
and my eyes were glazed and red.
My binder left a three-ring
indentation in my head.

I slept through class, and probably
I would have slept some more,
except my students woke me
as they headed out the door.

Kenn Nesbitt

3 **Listen to the groups present the poem. Talk about:**

- how the presenters showed their ideas about the character in the poem.
- what went well and what could be improved.

Thinking time

Reflect on what you have read in the last three weeks. Tell your partner what you enjoyed and didn't enjoy reading. Give reasons for your choices.

Listen to poems and interviews with poets online.

- Which poems did you enjoy?
- Which poet would you like to know more about?

3 Hair-raising stories

Using verbs and adverbs

1 Using the grammar boxes below and on the next page, see how quickly you can do the 'Gruesome grammar quiz'. Your teacher will time you. Get set, go!

- **a** Write down the verb in the following sentence: *A poor widow lived in a hut.*

- **b** Is the following sentence in the past, present or future tense? *They pulled her up.*

- **c** Find the auxiliary verb in the following sentence: *She is growing her hair.*

- **d** Correct the following sentence: *She chop wood in the forest.*

- **e** Add a verb to the following sentence: *Tomorrow, we _____ _____ to school.*

- **f** Is, was or were? *If I _____ a writer, I would write funny stories.*

- **g** Find the adverb in the following sentence: *The class sang loudly.*

- **h** What kind of adverb is the one in question **g**?

- **i** How many adverbs are there in the following sentence: *They ran to school very quickly.*

- **j** Add an adverb of time to the following sentence: *_____ I went to see my friend.*

Pens down. Well done!

Verbs

A **verb** is an action or doing word.

For example: He <u>eats</u> spaghetti. She <u>is walking</u> to school.

- <u>is</u> is the auxiliary verb.
- <u>walking</u> is the present participle.

Verbs can be more than one word.

Adverbs

Adverbs tell you more about verbs. Adverbs of:

- place tell you *where*, for example: She ran <u>home</u>.
- time tell you *when*, for example: She ran <u>yesterday</u>.
- manner tell you *how*, for example: She ran <u>quickly</u>.
- degree can tell you more about verbs or adjectives. They tell you by how much something happened, for example: She ran <u>very</u> quickly.

2 **Verbs need to agree with their subjects in number and person. Fix the errors so the sentences below are in Standard English.**

For example:
    He have short hair.
    He has short hair. (singular subject; singular verb)

a A poor widow live in a village.

b The villagers all draws their water from a well.

c The widow and her son chops wood every day in the forest.

d They uses the wood to make fires to cook their food.

e Her son are going away, so she must find her own wood.

f She chop some wood from the Iroko tree.

g This are a magic tree and people is not supposed to harm it.

h Everyone know this.

Thinking deeper

Sometimes the subject of a sentence can be a group of words.

<u>A group of players</u> is on the field. (group is the subject, and it is singular)

Complete the sentences below.

1 Neither of us _____ going to the meeting at break.

2 Fish and chips _____ my favourite food.

3 Everyone _____ waiting for him to arrive.

4 The whole class _____ in detention this afternoon.

Listening and speaking

1 **Different countries and cultures have their own folk tales and myths about why things came to be the way they are. Listen to the beginning of the following folk tale from Nigeria about why women have long hair.**

Folk tales

Folk tales are traditional fictional stories. They:

- were not written down in the past and so were originally spoken rather than read.
- teach a lesson.
- have a simple structure.

Why women have long hair

In the days when women had short hair just like men, there lived a poor widow called Bisi in a little hut in a village close to the forest.

Every evening the women of the village went in a long line through part of the forest, singing with water-pots on their heads to draw water from a well some distance away. Bisi went with them and when she returned home she would light a fire in front of her hut, put on a pot and cook the evening meal for herself and her son.

But one evening when it was time to make the fire, she found that she had no wood. So she ran to the next hut and asked for a few sticks, but her neighbour had none to spare and, in fact, though she asked in every hut nobody could give her wood to make a fire.

"Well," said Bisi, "I shall have to go to the forest and cut some wood myself because my son is away."

She took an axe and went into the forest, but she was very angry at having to waste so much time just when she should have been preparing the meal.

The first tree she cut down was the Iroko, which is a magic tree and must never be cut down.

"I don't care," thought Bisi. "I will cut off these low branches and chop them into sticks so that no one will know I have touched the magic tree.

In haste she did so, and soon returned to the village carrying a large bundle of sticks with which she made a roaring fire and cooked a savoury stew for her supper.

Then she went to sleep and forgot all about the wood she had cut, though the wise men declare that: "He who harms the Iroko tree will meet with sorrow in return."

② **GROUP WORK. What do you think is going to happen next?**

- Decide on what you think the ending of the story is going to be. Remember the title and personality of characters gives you clues too.
- Report back to the class. Which group has the most interesting ending?

PAIR WORK. Read the rest of the Nigerian folk tale.

Next evening the women went as usual along the forest-path to the well and Bisi went with them.

But as she passed by the Iroko tree, a hole suddenly appeared in the ground under Bisi's feet and she felt herself falling.

"Help me! Save me!" she cried and the other women all dropped their water-pots and rushed to her, seizing hold of her by the hair just as she was disappearing.

They pulled and pulled but Bisi continued to sink and so her hair grew longer and longer. At last, when her hair was almost a yard long they gave an extra hard tug and managed to pull her up out of the hole.

Then they collected their water-pots and ran back to the village as fast as they could. Bisi ran the fastest of all, but when they questioned her she was forced to confess that she had chopped some branches from the magic tree to make a fire.

"You have been very wicked, Bisi," said the Chief of the village, "but the Iroko has punished you sufficiently by making your hair grow so ridiculously long."

Everyone laughed at her and for a long time she was ashamed of her long hair. But one day, looking at herself in a pool of water she found that her hair was beautiful, so she twined flowers and ornaments into it and was very proud, forgetting it was a punishment.

Then the other women grew jealous and they all wished for long hair. At last they all agreed to dig a deep hole and each of them in turn jumped in while the rest held her by the hair until her tresses were stretched to a great length.

In the evening they all returned to the village rejoicing, with long hair twined with flowers and gold ornaments.

And since that time, all women have had long hair.

1 **Write the answers to the questions below.**

a Where did Bisi live?

b What did Bisi do every evening?

c What happened one evening?

d Why did she get angry?

e What solution did she find to her problem?

f How was Bisi punished for her deed?

g Write down the proverb that the wise men say.

h What did the Chief and the villagers think of Bisi's hair at first?

i How did their opinion change?

j What do you think of the ending of the story?

2 **Find the following parts of speech below in the story.**

a Find two verbs, two nouns and two adjectives in the sentence below.

   She made a roaring fire and cooked a savoury stew.

b Find an adverb in the sentence below.

   A hole suddenly appeared in the ground.

c What kind of adverb is in the sentence below?

   She ran fast carrying her water-pot.

d Complete the collective noun from the text.

   She was carrying a _____ of sticks.

e Replace two proper nouns in the sentence below with pronouns.

   One evening, Bisi found that Bisi had no wood.

f Find two adverbs in the sentence below. Say what kind they are.

   Your hair has grown so ridiculously long.

g Complete the sentence below from the text with adverbial phrases.

   _____ (time) the women went _____ (mannor) _____ _____ (plaoo) and Bioi went with them.

Adverbial phrases

Adverbial phrases tell you more about <u>verbs</u>.
Adverbial phrases of:

● place tell you *where*

● time tell you *when*

● manner tell you *how*

For example:
Every evening the women of the village <u>went</u> *in a long row, singing, through part of the forest*, **with water-pots on their heads**, <u>to draw</u> water *from a well some distance away*.

3 Read the words on the trees.

a Find the words on the tree below in the text and read them in context.

b Match the words on the trees to those of similar meaning.

c Write sentences that include as many of the words as possible.

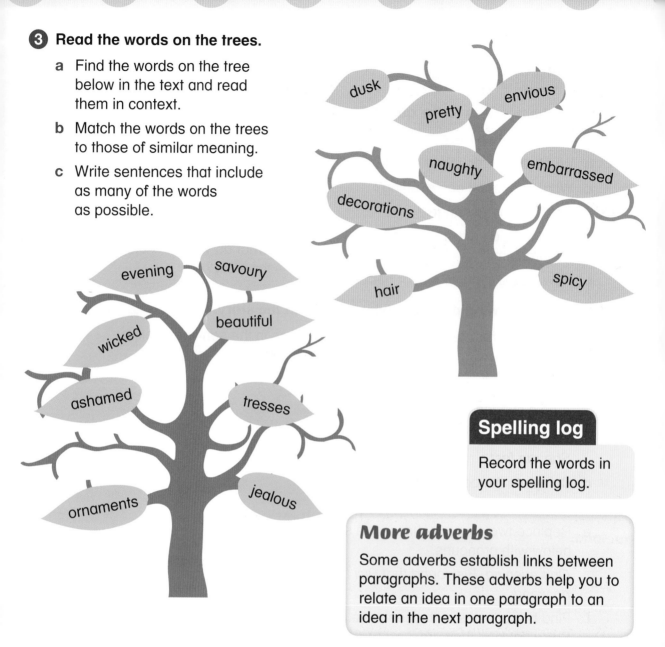

Spelling log

Record the words in your spelling log.

More adverbs

Some adverbs establish links between paragraphs. These adverbs help you to relate an idea in one paragraph to an idea in the next paragraph.

4 Below are some useful linking adverbs and phrases.

firstly	secondly	next
after	then	finally
before	first of all	the following day
the next evening	to begin with	since then
in summary	to conclude	

Find adverbs and phrases that link paragraphs in the folk tale *Why women have long hair*.

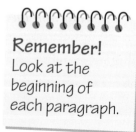

Remember!
Look at the beginning of each paragraph.

Writing

A summary is a simple, shortened account. Write a summary of the folk tale *Why women have long hair.* Use adverbs to make your summary flow from one idea to the next.

Reading and speaking

PAIR WORK. The story of *Rapunzel* is a traditional Western fairy tale. Scan the first verse on page 36 and talk about the questions below.

a How do you know *Rapunzel* is going to be a traditional fairy tale? (Think about how it begins.)

b What is different about the way the tale is presented?

c How many voices or speakers are there?

d Why do you think there two different voices?

e What is the second speaker's opinion about the setting?

Listening and reading

PAIR WORK. Listen to the fairy tale. Then read the tale out loud.

a Try out different voices for the different characters.

b What kind of person do you think each of the voices would be?

c What movements and gestures can you add to convey ideas about the characters?

d Read accurately and confidently.

Fairy tales

Fairy tales are fictional stories. They are characterised by:

• being set in imaginary places.

• magical elements.

• good and evil characters.

Once upon a time, in a land
far away.

Never very specific are they?

There was a wicked witch who
lived in a castle.

Of course there was, get on with it.

And in her garden grew the most
delicious herb in the world.

*Go on, go on, tell us about the
wall then!*

And it was surrounded by a high,
high wall.

*I should write these blooming
things myself.*

Now there was a man whose wife
longed to taste this delicious herb.

*Ha! Show me a man about to get
into big, big trouble!*

And she begged and pleaded, so in
spite of his fear, he climbed the wall.

Idiot.

And brought her the rampion.
She loved it so much, she asked
for more.

*Oh, what a surprise! I wonder
what he did then?*

So he mastered his fear, and
returned time again, for more
delicious rampion.

*Idiot x2. Something bad is going
to happen.*

One day the witch caught him,
and he begged for the rampion
and his life.

*And blamed it on the wife,
of course.*

And she let him go, on condition
that he brought her his new
born baby.

*For some lousy herbs?
Ridiculous!*

Which he duly did, so his
wife could continue to eat the
delicious rampion.

*Not sure I can listen to this
rubbish anymore.*

And the witch called the girl
Rapunzel, and locked her in a
tall tower.

*And they call this a story
for children?*

Rapunzel grew more beautiful by
the day, and her hair grew longer
and longer.

*Long golden tresses? That's more
like it!*

And when the witch wanted to
see her, she called, "Rapunzel let
down your hair!"

Bit rude, that, isn't it mate?

"That I may climb the golden
stair" and she climbed up her
hair to visit her.

*Where's the prince? Isn't there a
prince in this story?*

One day the king's son rode
by the tower, and heard
Rapunzel singing.

So I was right then!

And he fell in love and wanted to
climb up the tower and see this
beautiful girl.

*Don't stop now, what
happens next?*

by Fiona Macgregor

Reading, writing and speaking

1 **PAIR WORK. Read the summary in the box below about what happens next.**

- Write the lines of the other speaker in the fairy tale dialogue below. Choose words that express the speaker's opinions about the setting and characters. Your teacher will give you a worksheet with the words printed on it. Write the words for every other line.

What happens next?

The prince copied the witch and called, "Rapunzel let down your hair."

He climbed up to see her.

He visited Rapunzel every day until the witch found out.

In a rage, she cut off Rapunzel's hair and sent her to live in the wilderness.

The next time the prince visited, the witch lowered Rapunzel's plaits to him.

When he jumped on the balcony she attacked him fiercely.

He fell off the tower into a bed of thorns and they pierced his eyes.

Blind, and sad, he wandered for years through the wilderness.

Until one day, he heard a beautiful voice singing. "Rapunzel," he shouted.

She found him, and her tears fell on his eyes, and they grew clear again.

And he led her to his kingdom where they lived happily ever after.

2 **Check your writing carefully before you hand it in.**

- Is everything correctly spelled?
- Is the text correctly punctuated (full stops, capital letters)?
- Are there any errors of concord?

3 **Act out the end of your story for the rest of the class. You can read from your script – you don't have to know the lines off by heart.**

Spelling and vocabulary

Suffixes

A **suffix** is a small piece that you add to the end of a word, which changes its meaning or function. You can make an adverb by adding –*ly* to an adjective.

For example: quick – quickly

beautiful – beautifully

happy – happily (note the spelling: add 'i' if the word ends on *y*)

1 **Change the words in the box to adverbs.**

quick   careful   hungry   loud   tight   bad   imaginative   sad

2 **Now add each of your new adverbs to one of the sentences below.**

a That story was very _____ written. I liked it.

b "Move _____ over this rocky ground, everyone!" the teacher said.

c My brother played his music so _____ that the police came!

d Her hair was very _____ braided; it was pulled right back from her face.

e The class looked at the giant pizza _____.

f My father looked _____ at my new haircut. "Why?" he asked.

g The team ran _____ onto the field before the bell rang.

h That test went very _____ for me; I think I failed.

Adverbs of degree

Adverbs of degree can tell you more about an action, an adjective or another adverb. Adverbs have degrees of comparison.

Adverb	Comparative	Superlative
high	higher	highest
carefully	more carefully	most carefully
badly	worse	worst

3 **Read the sentence below from *Rapunzel*.**

Rapunzel grew more beautiful by the day, and her hair grew longer and longer.

  a Write down the adverbs of degree.

  b Which actions do they tell you about?

4 **Complete the sentences with the correct form of the adverb in brackets.**

  a Delicious herbs grew _____ in the witch's garden. (wild)

  b The man saw his wife grow _____ and _____ every day. (sad)

  c He could climb _____ than his wife. (high)

  d He climbed the wall _____ than his wife. (careful)

  e His wife loved the herb _____ than any other herb. (much)

  f Rapunzel's hair grew _____ and _____. (long)

  g The witch attacked the prince _____. (fierce)

  h The prince wandered _____ through the wilderness. (aimless)

5 **Copy and complete the chart.**

Adverb	Comparative	Superlative
quickly		
	softer	
		most rapidly
		tightest
	more recently	
hard		
	more fearfully	
		the least

GROUP WORK. Read the text below and talk about the pictures.

a Which hairstyle do you like? Give a reason.

b Does your hairstyle affect what people think of you? Give **one** reason for your answer.

Hairstyles

Hair can be cut, curled, straightened, coloured, extended or shaved right off. In Africa, hair braiding and hair cutting is an ancient tradition. If you want braids, the hairdresser ties long pieces of plaited hair into natural hair. Braids can be arranged in different styles, or have beads tied into them. Hairdressers can also arrange short hair into neat patterns, or cornrows.

Dreadlocks are coils that form naturally in curly hair if it is not cut or brushed for a long time. People rub the hair between their hands to make the coils more matted.

African barbershop signs are famous all over the world. You can see signs like these in many museums.

Braids can be used to create a number of different styles.

Writing

Design a hairstyle. Draw, label and caption your hairstyle. Then write three short paragraphs about your hairstyle.

Thinking time

Which folk tales and fairy tales have you read? Which is your most and least favourite? Why?

4 Reading a classic: *Alice in Wonderland*

1 Look at the book covers below. In which book will you find:

a a play?

b factual information?

c a story?

A
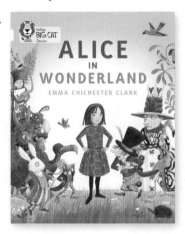

B
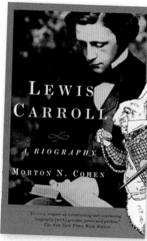

C

2 GROUP WORK. Talk about which book you think you would enjoy the most and why.

3 The Dewey decimal system is used to organise books in a library. Look at the following chart that shows a section of the Dewey decimal system.

a What numbers would you look for if you wanted to find the books shown above?

b Do research to find the numbers of the book you could not find on the chart.

820	English and Old English literatures
820	English & Old English (Anglo-Saxon) literatures
821	English poetry
822	English drama
823	English fiction
824	English essays
825	English speeches
826	English letters
827	English humour & satire
828	English miscellaneous writings
829	Old English (Anglo-Saxon) literature

Speaking and reading

1 GROUP WORK. Talk about what you know about the story *Alice in Wonderland*.

2 Read the beginning of *Alice in Wonderland*. This text is an adaptation of the original story written by Lewis Carroll 150 years ago.

> **Fantasy fiction**
> Fantasy stories usually include:
> - an imaginary setting.
> - good and bad characters.
> - talking animals.
> - magic.

Alice was sitting with her sister on the riverbank. She'd never felt so bored. There was nothing to do. She'd half thought of making a daisy chain, but couldn't be bothered to get up and pick the daisies. Her sister's book looked duller than dull. "What's the use of a book," thought Alice, "without pictures or conversation?" But at that moment a white rabbit with pink eyes and a jacket to match rushed by. "Oh, dear! Oh, dear! I'll be late!" he said as he looked at his pocket watch. Alice leapt up and ran after him, just as he disappeared down a rabbit hole. Suddenly she was

falling …

falling …

and falling …

Down …

down …

down she fell,

quite slowly, looking at shelves all around her as she went. She seemed to be falling forever and was just wondering if she was anywhere near the centre of the earth, when she landed – thump! – on a pile of dry leaves.

The White Rabbit rushed ahead down a long, dark passage. "Oh, my ears and whiskers!" he muttered. "How late it's getting."

Alice raced after him, but he completely vanished, and she found herself alone in a long hall with doors on either side. Every door was locked. How was she to get out again?

Comprehension

GROUP WORK. First talk about the answers to the questions below. Then write the answers.

a Where is the beginning of the story set?

b Where is the next part of the story set?

c Why do you think 'falling' and 'down' are written as they are?

d How do you know that Alice felt lazy?

e What does the dialogue of the rabbit tell you about his character?

f How do you think Alice feels after she falls down?

g What do you think happens next?

h How do you think Alice gets out?

Reading and writing

1 **PAIR WORK. Read the short biography about Lewis Carroll on the right. Then ask your partner questions about it.**

Biographies

A biography is a non-fiction account of someone's life, written by someone else. They:

• are written in the past tense.

• use time connectives to link ideas.

• give events in chronological order.

• link dates and events.

• sometimes include headings, subheadings, timelines, bullet points, photographs and captions.

2 **Use the internet and other resources to research and write a short biography about one of your favourite writers.**

Birth name: Charles L Dodgson

Pen name: Lewis Carroll

Born: 27 January 1832 in Daresbury, England

Died: 14 January 1898 (aged 65) in Guildford, Surrey, England

Education: Rugby School, University of Oxford

Occupation: Writer, illustrator, poet, mathematician, photographer, teacher

Notable works: *Alice's Adventures in Wonderland, Through the Looking-Glass, The Hunting of the Snark, Jabberwocky*

Interesting information:

• Lewis Carroll had a bad stammer except when he was speaking to young children.

• He loved to entertain children with fantastic stories of dream worlds.

• He first told the story of *Alice's Adventures in Wonderland* (commonly shortened to *Alice in Wonderland*) to Alice Liddell and her two sisters while at a picnic. Alice told him to write the story down.

• The book *Alice's Adventures in Wonderland* was first published in 1865 and by the time Lewis Carroll died, it was one of the most popular books in the world.

1 GROUP WORK. Later in Unit 4, your group is going to perform a short play. Each person will either act or help backstage. Begin your preparation now.

- Read about the people behind the scenes in a play.
- Talk about who in your group would be best at each job.
- Remember to listen to each other and give everyone a chance to speak.

The Props Manager:

- finds properties (props) that are needed to stage the play, for example: a table, a plate of tarts, chairs and so on.
- makes sure the props are on stage at the right time and in the right place for each performance.

The Costume Manager:

- decides what the characters will wear in each scene.
- finds or makes the clothes for each character.

The Stage Manager:

- oversees all the action backstage.
- tells the cast when it's their cue.

The Lighting and Sound Manager:

- is responsible for sound effects.
- lights the stage.
- sometimes uses a spotlight to follow the main character.

The Director studies the script and decides:

- how the play will be staged.
- how the characters will say their lines.
- how the characters will move on stage.

2 Write lists to explain what the people below do in a play.

- choreographer
- make-up artist

Vocabulary

1 Find the acting terms in the information on page 44 and read them in context. Match the terms to their meanings. Use a dictionary or an online tool to help you.

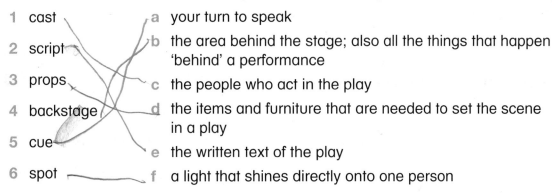

1 cast   a   your turn to speak

2 script   b   the area behind the stage; also all the things that happen 'behind' a performance

3 props   c   the people who act in the play

4 backstage   d   the items and furniture that are needed to set the scene in a play

5 cue   e   the written text of the play

6 spot   f   a light that shines directly onto one person

2 There are many words in drama that look the same as other words but have different meanings.

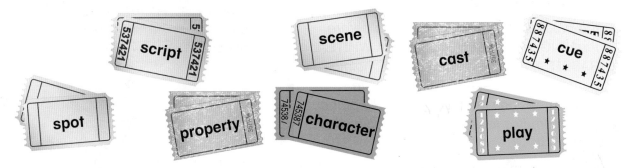

a   Use your dictionary or a thesaurus to find two meanings for each of the words.

b   Then make sentences with each word to show you understand its meaning.

3 Say the words below out loud.

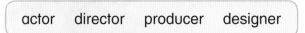

a   What do you notice about the sound at the end?

Now say the words below out loud.

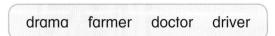

b   What is common about the end sounds?

c   Try saying the different set of sounds below that share the same ending sound.

> city   valley   coffee   quickly   happily   Betty   Mary   Tony

Spelling log

Record any interesting words in your spelling log.

Reading and speaking

GROUP WORK. Read the script for *Who stole the tarts?* Each person reads a part.

Who stole the tarts?

The courtroom. The KING and QUEEN of hearts sit on thrones. ALICE, THE MARCH HARE, DORMOUSE and BIRDS, ANIMALS and a PACK OF CARDS watch the proceedings. A KNAVE stands before the KING and QUEEN in chains. A WHITE RABBIT stands before the KNAVE holding a trumpet and a scroll. JURORS write their names on slates. In the middle of the courtroom is a table with a large dish of tarts on it.

(WHITE RABBIT blows his trumpet.)

RABBIT: (*Shouting*) Silence in court!

KING: (*Pompously*) Herald, read the accusation!

RABBIT: (*Reading the scroll.*)
The Queen of Hearts, she made some tarts,
All on a summer day:
The Knave of Hearts, he stole those tarts,
And took them quite away!

KING: Call the first witness to the stand!

RABBIT: First witness!

(MAD HATTER enters wearing a large hat and takes the stand. He holds a cup of tea in one hand and a piece of bread in the other.)

KING: Take off your hat!

MAD HATTER: (*Nervously*) It ... it ... it isn't mine.

KING:	(*Exclaiming*) Stolen!
MAD HATTER:	(*Shaking with fright*) No! No! I sell them. I'm a hatter.

(MAD HATTER *takes a bite of his teacup instead of his bread.*)

KING:	Give your evidence.
MAD HATTER:	(*Trembling*) I'm a poor man, your Majesty … and I hadn't begun my tea … not above a week or so … and what with the bread and butter getting so thin … and the twinkling of the tea …
KING:	(*Confused*) The twinkling of what?
MAD HATTER:	It began with the tea.
KING:	(*Angrily*) Of course twinkling begins with a T! Do you take me for a dunce? Go on!
MAD HATTER:	I'm a poor man and most things twinkled after that … only the March Hare said …
MARCH HARE:	I didn't!
MAD HATTER:	You did!
MARCH HARE:	I deny it!
KING:	He denies it. Leave that part out.
MAD HATTER:	Well at any rate, the Dormouse said … and after that I cut some bread.
JUROR:	What did the Dormouse say?
MAD HATTER:	I can't remember.
KING:	You must remember or I'll have you executed!
MAD HATTER:	(*Dropping his teacup and bread.*) I'm a poor man …
KING:	(*Looking irritated*) You're a very poor speaker. Sit down if that is all you know.
QUEEN:	Just take his head off outside!

(MAD HATTER *rushes out of sight before anyone can get him.*)

KING:	Call the next witness!
RABBIT:	Second witness!

(COOK *takes the stand.*)

KING:	Give your evidence.
COOK:	Shan't!
KING:	What are the tarts made of?
COOK:	Pepper.
DORMOUSE:	(*Sleepily*) Treacle.

QUEEN:	(*Shrieking*) Off with his whiskers!
KING:	Call the next witness!
RABBIT:	Alice!

(COOK *leaves the stand.* ALICE *who has suddenly begun growing, jumps up and tips over the jury box.*)

| ALICE: | (*Apologetically*) Sorry. |

(*Everyone in court makes a noise. The* JURORS *get back onto their seats and reorganise themselves while Alice takes the stand.*)

KING:	Silence! Rule 42! All those more than a kilometre high must leave court!
ALICE:	(*Indignantly*) I'm not a kilometre high!
KING:	Let the jury consider the verdict!
QUEEN:	No! No! Sentence first, verdict after!
ALICE:	Rubbish!
QUEEN:	(*Turning purple with rage.*) Hold your tongue!
ALICE:	I won't!
QUEEN:	(*Yelling at the top of her voice.*) Off with her head!
ALICE:	Whatever. I'm not scared of you. You're just a pack of cards.

(*Pack of cards descends on* ALICE *while she tries to beat them off, half laughing, half crying.*)

The end

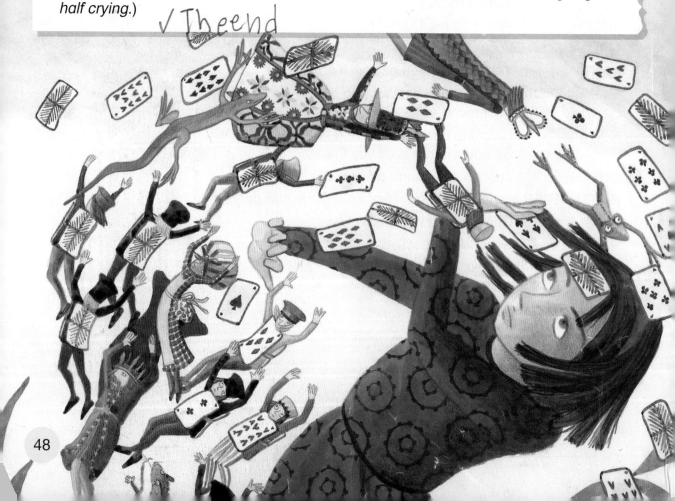

Listening and speaking

Plan, practise, present and then assess your performance of the play
Who stole the tarts?

1 **GROUP WORK. Decide who will take which role backstage. Talk about what needs to be done. Make notes of what your jobs are.**

- Props manager will collect the items you need.
- Costume manager will find the costumes.
- Lights and sound manager will use a spot (torch) to light the main characters, and make sound effects.
- Stage manager will organise rehearsals, cues, and manage practices.
- Director will direct the show.

2 **The director gives out roles to each person. Read the playscript again in your allocated roles.**

3 **Talk about how you are going to act out the play.**

The director has the final say, but everyone should share ideas about how to stage the performance. Backstage people should write down what is needed for each section of the play.

4 **Think about which non-verbal communication techniques you will use to enhance your performance.**

5 **Perform your plays for your classmates.**

Reading and speaking

1 Read the opening of the following playscript. It is a musical of *Alice in Wonderland*, written by Henry Savile Clarke.

2 Talk about the features of a script. Answer the questions.

a Where is the opening scene set?

b Who are the characters?

c What do the stage directions tell you about the main characters?

Play title

Stage directions at the beginning of the scene are in italics and written in the present tense.

Stage directions within each scene are in italics, and in brackets.

'The characters' names are in capital letters. Today, we put a colon after each name.

Dialogue without speech marks

ALICE IN WONDERLAND.

ACT I.

SCENE.—*A Forest in Autumn.   Alice asleep at foot of tree and Fairies dancing round her.*

CHORUS OF FAIRIES.

Sleep, maiden, sleep ! as we circle around thee,
    Lulled by the music of bird and of bee,
Safe in the forest since fairies have found thee
    Here where we come to keep tryst by the tree.
Sleep, Alice, sleep ! these are magical numbers,
    Songs that we learnt from the mount and the
        stream.
Ours be the task to keep watch o'er thy slumbers,
    Wake, Alice, wake to the Wonderland dream.

[*Fairies troop off at each side, the Chorus dying softly away in the distance.   Scene changes to Wonderland, Garden set.   The CATERPILLAR discovered smoking on gigantic mushroom at side. ALICE wakes up, and goes up and down stage in great bewilderment.   The white RABBIT crosses the stage hurriedly.*

RABBIT. Oh! the Duchess, the Duchess ! Oh, won't she be savage if I've kept her waiting !
ALICE. If you please, Sir—(RABBIT *starts and exit dropping white kid gloves and fan.*) Dear ! Dear ! How queer everything is to-day. And yesterday things went on just as usual. I wonder if I've been changed in the night. Let me think, was I the same when I got up this morning. But if I'm not the same who am I ? Ah ! that's the puzzle. I'll try if I know all the things I used to know.

Writing

**PAIR WORK. Write the first ten lines of your own playscript.
Set the scene and introduce the main characters.**

Listening and speaking

1 **In *Alice in Wonderland* a lot of things do not make sense. Listen to the strange experience Alice has at a tea party.**

2 **GROUP WORK. Talk about what you have heard.**

   a What is the setting?

   b Which characters are part of the scene?

   c Describe the personality of each character.

   d Talk about the relationship between the Dormouse, and the Hatter and Hare.

Reading and speaking

Talk about the questions when you have watched the film *Alice in Wonderland*.

a Did Alice look and sound like you expected her to?

b What do you think of the setting of the film?

c Which visual parts did you like? Why?

d How did the film differ to the story you listened to?

e Read the comments that some children wrote after watching Tim Burton's version of the film. Do you agree or disagree with their opinions? Why?

f What comment would you write about the film?

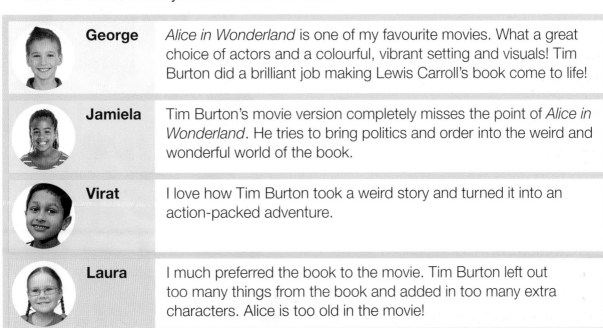

	George	*Alice in Wonderland* is one of my favourite movies. What a great choice of actors and a colourful, vibrant setting and visuals! Tim Burton did a brilliant job making Lewis Carroll's book come to life!
	Jamiela	Tim Burton's movie version completely misses the point of *Alice in Wonderland*. He tries to bring politics and order into the weird and wonderful world of the book.
	Virat	I love how Tim Burton took a weird story and turned it into an action-packed adventure.
	Laura	I much preferred the book to the movie. Tim Burton left out too many things from the book and added in too many extra characters. Alice is too old in the movie!

Reading and writing

1 **Read the interview with Alice below. Turn the sentences into direct speech.**

Start like this:

The interviewer said, "Alice, ...

An unwelcome guest

Interview with Alice

INTERVIEWER: Alice, tell us what happened that day.

ALICE: I saw a long table where the March Hare and the Hatter were sitting having a tea party.

INTERVIEWER: Was anyone else at the tea party?

ALICE: Only the Dormouse, who was fast asleep.

INTERVIEWER: Did they invite you to join them for tea?

ALICE: No, they did not!

INTERVIEWER: Why not?

ALICE: They are very rude!

INTERVIEWER: What did they say?

ALICE: They lied and said there was no room for me at the table.

INTERVIEWER: What did you do?

ALICE: I sat down because there was plenty of room!

INTERVIEWER: What happened then?

Direct speech

Direct speech shows what someone is saying.

For example: ALICE: That was a strange tea party.

Alice said, "That was a strange tea party."

- Add the word 'said'.
- Use a comma after 'said'.
- The spoken words and their punctuation go inside inverted commas.

Thinking deeper

If a writer didn't use speech marks in a story, how else could they show where speech begins and ends? Experiment with some ideas. Write a short story and give to your partner to read. How did they manage? What feedback did they give you?

2 Imagine you are the interviewer. Write five questions you would ask Alice.

3 Change the sentences below from direct to reported speech. Replace the word 'said' in each of the sentences with a different word.

a The Mad Hatter said, "Alice, you must go for a haircut tomorrow."

b Alice said, "I will not go."

c The Mad Hatter said, "Yesterday I sang to the queen."

d Alice said, "I am sure the queen enjoyed hearing the song."

e The Mad Hatter said, "She threatened to cut off my head."

f Alice said, "I think the queen is mean."

g The Mad Hatter said, "Today I will make up a new song."

h Alice said, "I can help you write it down now."

i The Mad Hatter said, "Thank you, I appreciate it."

j Alice asked, "What shall we write about?"

Reported speech

Reported speech tells you what someone has said. It is in the past tense because it is reporting what has been said.

For example: Alice said, "I am going to a tea party today."

Alice said that she was going to a tea party that day.

Changing **direct** to **reported speech**:

- Add 'that'.
- The tense changes to the past tense.
- The pronoun changes.
- Time words also change, because you are telling about something in the past.

this day	that day
today	that day
tomorrow	the next day
yesterday	the day before/ the previous day
now	then

4 What other words can you use instead of 'said'? Make a list.

Reading and speaking

Read the poem 'How Doth the Little Crocodile', which Alice recites in *Alice's Adventures in Wonderland*. Then talk about the questions below.

a Which features describe the crocodile?

b How does the crocodile hide his real intentions?

c Which words make the crocodile seem human?

d Imagine that the crocodile is a real person. What sort of personality does he have?

e Which words convey mood in the poem?

f What is the rhyming pattern?

g Make up a moral for the poem.

Poetry

'How Doth the Little Crocodile' is a poem that includes:

- a simple rhyme scheme.
- rhythm.
- parody.
- personification.
- assonance.
- adjectives.

*How doth the little crocodile
Improve his shining tail,
And pour the waters of the Nile
On every golden scale!*

*How cheerfully he seems to grin
How neatly spreads his claws,
And welcomes little fishes in
With gently smiling jaws!*

Writing

Write a poem that has similar features to 'How Doth the Little Crocodile'.

- Choose an animal to write about.
- Give your poem a title.
- Begin each verse with 'How'.
- Include personification.
- Use words that convey mood.
- Include rhythm and rhyme.

Remember!

Personification is when a thing or an idea is given human qualities.

Thinking time

Did you prefer the story, the play or the film of *Alice in Wonderland*? Why?

5 Songs of the sea

Vocabulary

1 **Write the words below in alphabetical order.**

> early   enter   eerie   enterprising   end   eye

2 **Look up the words below in a dictionary.**

disturbance   indelibly

phenomenon   triumphant

enterprising   communicated

passive

a Write down their meanings.

b Learn the words for a spelling test.

Thinking deeper

You can break each word down into smaller sections, to make it easier to say. These small sections are called **syllables**. Each syllable has a vowel sound in it.

For example: dis/tur/bance

Try the other words in the list.

Spelling log

Record the words in your spelling log.

Reading

Listen to the text below from the fantasy fiction book _The Whale Rider_. Then read the text silently.

Text 1

Not long after Kahu's dive for the stone, in the early hours of the morning, a young man was jogging along Wainui Beach, not far from Whangara, when he noticed a great disturbance on the sea. "The horizon all of a sudden got lumpy," he said as he tried to describe the phenomenon, "and lumps were moving in a solid mass to the Beach." As he watched, the jogger realised that he was witnessing the advance to the beach of a herd of whales. "They kept coming and coming," he told the _Gisborne Herald_, "and they didn't turn away. I ran down to the breakwater. All around me the

whales were stranding themselves. They were whistling an eerie haunting sound. Every now and then they would spout. I felt like crying."

The news was quickly communicated to the town, and the local radio and television stations sent reporters out to Wainui. One enterprising cameraman hired a local helicopter to fly him over the scene. It is his flickering film images that most of us remember. In the early morning light, along three kilometres of coastland, are two hundred whales, male, female, young, waiting to die. The waves break over them and hiss around their passive frames. Dotted on the beach are human shapes, drawn to the tragedy. The pilot of the helicopter says on camera, "I've been to Vietnam, y'know and I've done deer culling down south." His lips are trembling and his eyes are moist with tears. "But my oath, this is like seeing the end of the world."

Comprehension

Answer the questions below.

a Which words in the text give you a clue about where the story is happening?

b What are the 'lumps on the horizon' that the young jogger sees?

c To whom did he tell his story?

d Give a quote from the text that tells how he felt about what he was seeing.

e How did the rest of the world get to know about this?

f Why do you think the writer says 'human shapes' instead of 'people'?

g What are two other bad things the helicopter pilot has seen?

h What does 'zooms in' mean?

Listening and speaking

1 GROUP WORK. Discuss the questions below.

a When a herd of whales is stranded, what can people do about it?

b Why do you think some scientists believe that it is better to leave stranded whales alone? What do you think?

2 Choose two teams in the class and have a class debate about whether stranded whales should be helped or not. Look at the diagram on the next page to help you present your debate.

Remember!

When debating:

- your information must be easy to understand.
- convey ideas and opinions concisely.
- speak precisely.
- be aware of your audience.
- listen and respond to the viewpoints of others.

56

How to hold a debate

One side argues in favour.
They are the **proposition**.

The other side argues
against. They are the
opposition.

The chair introduces the
debate, keeps order, and
counts the vote.

The floor (the
audience).

Reading

Read the persuasive letter on the next page.

a   What is the purpose of the letter?

b   How does the writer express his viewpoint?

c   Which words convey feeling and mood?

d   Find one fact and one opinion in the letter.

Spelling log

Look up the meaning
of interesting or new
words and record them
in your spelling log.

Writing

**Write a letter to the *Gisborne Herald* giving your views about culling.
Choose words that convey your feelings and mood. Use the notes on
the next page to help you set out your letter correctly.**

Your address on the left-hand side

Leave a line

The date

Leave a line

The greeting

Leave a line

The topic of your letter – in bold if you are typing or underlined if you are handwriting

Opening statement expresses the viewpoint

Uses facts to support viewpoint

Connectives make logical conclusions

Rhetorical questions and repetition can be used for emphasis

Persuasive device

Leave a line

Yours faithfully

Sign your name

---

19 The Drive
Auckland
New Zealand
5565

19 March 2020

Dear Sir

Whaling is cruel

I believe that whaling is cruel and should be banned in all countries. In 1986, the International Whaling Commission (IWC) banned commercial whaling. So, why are some countries still killing whales?

I think that whaling continues in some countries because people are arrogant and greedy. They only think of themselves and making money, and not about what is good for our planet. Surely, people and nature can exist together in harmony. As a nation, we need to think long term. We need to protect our incredible planet for future generations.

We must work together to stop whaling. Let us use our powers of public persuasion to urge our president to talk to the leaders of countries that are still whaling. It is time to save our planet instead of destroying it.

Yours faithfully
M A Gallow
Matthew Gallow

Reading and speaking

1 Study the back cover of the book *The Whale Rider* carefully. Find the answers to the questions below.

a What is the story about?

b In which country is the book set?

c Who is the writer of the book?

d Which sentence shows that the book has been made into a film?

e How many awards has the film won?

2 Watch the film *Whale Rider*. Discuss the following questions.

a Did the main character look and sound as you expected her to?

b What did you think of the setting of the film?

c What did you think of the relationship between Kahu and her great-grandfather?

d Do you think traditions are important? Say why, or why not.

e What did you think of the ending of the film?

Eight-year-old Kahu craves her great-grandfather's love and attention. But he's focused on his duties as chief of a Maori tribe in Whangara, New Zealand – a tribe that claims descent from the legendary "whale rider". In every generation since the whale rider, a male has inherited the title of chief. But now there is no male heir – there's only Kahu. She should be next in line for the title, but her great-grandfather is blinded by tradition and sees no use for a girl.

Kahu will not be ignored. And in her struggle she has a unique ally: the whale rider himself, from whom she has inherited the ability to communicate with whales. Once that sacred gift is revealed, Kahu may be able to re-establish her people's ancestral connections, earn her great-grandfather's attention – and lead her tribe to a bold new future.

WITI IHIMAERA's sweeping story of love and destiny is the inspiration for the major motion picture *Whale Rider*, which won over 20 film awards, including the 2003 Sundance Film Festival World Cinema Audience Award, the 2002 Toronto International Film Festival People's Choice Award, and the 2003 BAFTA Children's Award for Best Film.

Writing

Write a review of the film *Whale Rider* for your local newspaper.

Film review

Title: ....

Actors: ....

Director: ....

Star rating: ☆ ☆ ☆ ☆ ☆

Short summary of what the film is about: ....

Your opinion of the film: ....

Why you recommend or don't recommend the film: ....

Using punctuation and sentence structures

1 **Match the punctuation symbol to its meaning.**

1 **,**

2 **.**

3 **?**

4 **!**

5 **" "**

a Shows strong feelings, emphasis and amusement, gives a command

b Shows a question

c Shows a pause, separates clauses, and separates items in a list

d Shows that those are someone's words

e Shows the end of a sentence

2 **Write the sentences below in Standard English by ordering the words correctly and adding punctuation.**

a wainui beach along was a young man jogging

b down the breakwater to I ran

c two hundred there are whales old ones young ones baby ones and

d the awful most thing it was ive ever seen my life in

e stop shouted he

f the reporters he told we watched from the helicopter the whole thing

3 **Find the subject, verb and object in the simple sentences below. Note: Always find the verb first; then the rest is easy!**

a Whales eat plankton.

b Journalists take photographs.

c An enterprising cameraman hired a helicopter.

d Our whole family likes spaghetti.

e The man stopped his work.

f All the children in the class did their homework.

Simple sentences

Simple sentences have:

● a subject (the person or thing doing the action).

● a verb (the action).

For example: **The girl sang.**

subject verb

People shouted.

subject verb

Most sentences also need: an object (the thing the action happens to).

For example: **We ate breakfast.**

subject verb object

They won the soccer match.

subject verb object

A subject or object does not have to be one word. It can be a phrase like 'the girls in Class 5', or 'the crowd on the beach'.

4 Give the sentences below suitable subjects. Then write the sentences.

a _____ noticed big lumps on the sea.

b _____ was on the radio.

c _____ ran down to the beach.

d _____ were whistling, an eerie haunting sound.

e _____ said, "I have never seen anything like this before."

f _____ zooms in on one of the whales.

g _____ smiled directly at the camera.

h _____ was very unhappy that night.

Compound sentences

A compound sentence is two simple sentences joined together.
Joining words are words like: *and, but, nor* and *or*. They are also
called **connectives**.

For example: They saw the whales. They rushed to the beach.
They saw the whales and they rushed to the beach.

Note: you could leave out the second 'they'; you don't have to repeat
the subject.

5 Say whether the sentences below are simple or compound. If they are compound sentences, write down the joining word.

a Kahu was a girl, but she dived for the stone anyway.

b Her great-grandfather was very angry.

c He was very traditional and he was fierce about his traditions.

d Kahu swims with the whales every day.

e Will Kahu be chief, or will her great-grandfather choose someone else?

f She loved the whales and she disobeyed him.

g Her father was furious, but her mother was not.

h The family was divided about the matter.

6 Join the simple sentences below to make compound sentences.
Use the connectives in brackets.

a Nobody saw her slip away. Nobody saw her enter the water. (and)

b The car lights shone on her white dress. The car lights shone on her head in the water. (and)

c I saw Kahu. I yelled, "Hey!" (and)

d A wave crashed on her. She kept on swimming. (but)

PAIR WORK. Practise reading the next text out loud. There are two voices in the text.

- First read the text together.
- Then decide who is going to read which voice.
- Practise reading the text aloud, so you can read it to the class.

moko: tattoo-like markings
'Karangi mai': 'Here, I am calling'
'Ko Kahutia Te Rangi?': 'Are you chief fish of the sea?'
'Ko Kahutia Te Rangi au': 'Yes, I am chief fish of the sea'
'Ko Paikea': 'Honoured sea god'

Text 2

Nobody saw her slip away and enter the water. Nobody knew at all until she was half way through the waves. Then the headlights and spotlights from the cars along the beach picked up her white dress and that little head bobbing up and down in the waves. As soon as I saw her, I knew it was Kahu.

"Hey!" I yelled. I pointed through the driving rain. Other spotlights began to catch her. In that white dress and white beribboned pigtails, she was like a small puppy, trying to keep its head up. A wave would crash over her, but somehow she would appear on the other side, gasping wide-eyed, and doing what looked like a cross between a dog paddle and a breast stroke.

Instantly I ran through the waves. People said I acted like a maniac. I plunged into the sea.
If the whale lives, we live. These were the only words Kahu could think of.

We have lost our way of talking to whales.

The water was freezing, but not to worry.

The waves were huge, but kei te pai. The rain was like spears, but hei aha.

Every now and then she had to take a deep breath because sometimes the waves were like dumpers, slamming her down to the sandy bottom, but somehow she bobbed right back up like a cork. Now the trouble was that the lights from the beach were dazzling her eyes, making it hard to see where she was going. Her neck was hurting with the constant looking up, but *there, there,* was the whale with the moko. She dog paddled purposefully towards it. A wave smashed into her and she swallowed more seawater. She began to cough and tread water. Then she set her face with determination. As she approached the whale, she suddenly remembered what she was supposed to do.

"Karanga mai, karanga mai, karanga mai." She raised her head and began to call to the whale.

The headlights and spotlights were dazzling upon the whale. It may have been the sudden light, or a cross current, but the eye of the whale seemed to flicker. Then the whale appeared to be looking at the young girl swimming.

Ko Kahutia Te Rangi?

"Kahu!" I could hear Granny Flowers screaming in the wind.

My boots were dragging me down. I had to stop and reach under to take them off. I looked up. I tried to see where Kahu was. The waves lifted me up and down.

"Kahu, no!" I cried.

She had reached the whale and was hanging onto its jaw.

"Help me," she cried. "Ko Kahutia Te Rangi au. Ko Paikea."

The whale shuddered at the words.

By chance, Kahu felt the whale's forward fin. Her fingers tightened quickly around it. She held on for dear life.

And the whale felt a surge of gladness which, as it mounted, became ripples of ecstasy, ever increasing. He began to communicate his joy to all parts of his body.

Out beyond the breakwater the herd suddenly became alert. With hope rising, they began to sing their encouragement to their leader.

She was going, our Kahu. She was going into the deep ocean. I could hear her small piping voice in the darkness as she left us.

She was going with the whales into the sea and the rain. She was a small figure in a white dress, kicking the whale as if it was a horse, her braids swinging in the rain. Then she was gone and we were left behind.

Ko Paikea, ko Paikea.

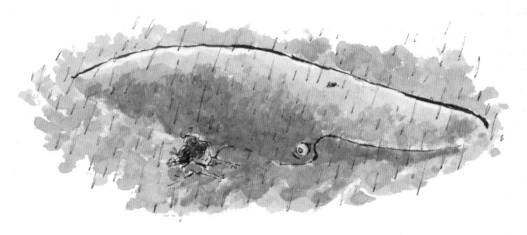

Vocabulary

Find words and sentences in the *The Whale Rider* texts that add feeling and mood.

a   How do the words make you feel?

b   What mood is created through the writer's choice of words?

c   Which words does the writer use in place of 'went' and 'go'? Why does he use them?

1 Listen for repetitive sounds as your teacher reads the poem *Sea Fever*.

Sea Fever

I must go down to the seas again, to the lonely sea
     and the sky
And all I ask is a tall ship, and a star to steer her by;
And the wheel's kick and the wind's song and the
     white sail's shaking
And a grey mist on the sea's face, and a grey
     dawn breaking.

I must go down to the seas again, for the call of the
     running tide
Is a wild call and a clear call that may not be denied;
And all I ask is a windy day with the white clouds flying,
And the flung spray and the blown spume, and the
     sea-gulls crying.

I must go down to the seas again, to the
     vagrant gypsy life,
To the gull's way and the whale's way where
     the wind's like a whetted knife;
And all I ask is a merry yarn from a laughing
     fellow-rover,
And quiet sleep and a sweet dream when the long
     trick's over.

John Masefield

Remember!

Alliteration is when you repeat a consonant sound.
the whale's way where the wind's like a whetted knife

Lyric poems

Lyric poems:
• express personal feelings.
• don't tell a story.
• have song-like qualities.
• often have a refrain repeated throughout the poem.

2 GROUP WORK. Discuss the poem.

a Find examples of the following figures of speech in the poem:
  alliteration   personification   simile

b Which words set a mood of adventure and freedom?

c Why do you think the poet begins every verse in the same way?

3 GROUP WORK. Sing the poem.

Thinking time

You have read texts from books written by the writers listed below.
• Hilary McKay
• Sharon Creech
• Louis Sachar
• Lewis Carroll
• Witi Ihimaera
Which is your favourite writer? Why?

6 Stories from around the world

Vocabulary

Spelling log

Record new words in your spelling log.

1 Use the suffixes in the box to make as many new words as you can from the root words.

beauty   invite   civilise   curious   hope

| –tion   –ful   –fully   –ed   –ly   –ity |

2 Choose three word families. Make a sentence with each word in the family to show you understand its meaning.

For example: The two of them were in **love**.

They had a **lovely** time at the picnic.

He came from a **loveless** home, which made him very sad.

3 Read the expressions below.

a Write down what you think each expression means.

b Look up one expression and be ready to tell the class where it comes from and what it means.

The face that launched a thousand ships

HOT AS HADES

Achilles' heel

The Midas touch

Reading and listening

Listen to the following text. Write down any words you don't understand. Look them up afterwards in your dictionary.

The text comes from a book called *Walk Two Moons*. The pupils have been given a project to research a myth and present it to the class. Phoebe is presenting the myth of 'Pandora's Box'.

> **Myths**
>
> Myths are made-up up stories. They:
> - are set a long time ago before stories were written down.
> - try to explain how the world works and how we should treat each other.

"As I was saying," Phoebe continued, "Zeus decided to give Man a lovely present, since Man seemed a little lonely down there on Earth, with only the animals to keep him company. So, Zeus made a sweet and beautiful woman, and then he invited all the Olympians to dinner. It was a very civilised dinner, with *matching plates.*"

Mary Lou and Ben exchanged an eyebrow message.

"At this civilised dinner, Zeus asked the Olympians to give the beautiful woman presents – to make her feel like a *welcome guest.*" Phoebe glanced at me. "They gave her all kinds of wonderful things: a fancy shawl, a silver dress, beauty —"

Ben interrupted. "I thought you said she was already beautiful."

"I *know.* They gave her *more* beauty. Are you satisfied?" Her lip was no longer trembling. Now she was blushing. "The Olympians also gave her the ability to sing, the power of persuasion, a gold crown, flowers and many truly wonderful things such as that. Because

of all these gifts, Zeus named her Pandora, which means 'the gift of all'."

Her heart attack was apparently subsiding. She was getting into it. "There were two other gifts that I have not mentioned yet. One of them was curiosity. That is why all women are curious, by the way, because it was a gift given to the very first woman."

Ben said, "I wish she had been given the gift of silence."

"As I was *saying,*" Phoebe continued, "Pandora was given curiosity. There was one more gift, too, and that was a beautiful box, covered in gold and jewels, *but* – and this is very important – she was forbidden to open the box."

Ben said, "Then why did they give it to her?"

He was beginning to irritate Phoebe, you could tell. She said, "That's what I'm telling you. It was a present."

"But why did they give her a present that she couldn't open?"

Phoebe looked puzzled. "I don't know. It's just in the story. As I was saying, Pandora was not supposed to open the box, but because she had been given ever so much curiosity, she really, really, really wanted to know what was inside, so one day, she opened the box."

"I knew it," Ben said. "I knew she was going to open the box the minute that you said she was not supposed to open it."

Misako raised her hand.

Phoebe sighed. "Do you have a question?"

"What is in the box?"

"As I was about to say, before Ben interrupted me, inside the box were all the evils in the world."

"What is evils?" Shigeru asked.

"As I was *about* to explain, inside the box were all the evils of the world such as hatred, envy, plagues, sickness, cholesterol …"

Mr Birkway scratched his head. He looked as if he might interrupt, but he didn't.

Phoebe continued. "There were brain tumours and sadness. There were lunatics and kidnapping and murders …" She glanced at Mr Birkway before rushing on, "… and all that kind of thing. Pandora tried to close the lid, she really tried when she saw all the horrible things rushing out of it, but she could not get it closed in time, and that is why there are all these evils in the world. There was only one good thing in the box."

"What was it?" asked Ben.

"As I was *about* to explain, the only good thing in the box was Hope."

"What is Hope?" Shigeru said.

"Hope?" Phoebe said. "Hmm Hope is … hope. It's hoping that … hmm. Hope is a little hard to explain."

"Try," said Mr Birkway.

Everyone was staring at Phoebe. "It is a feeling that — a wish that — something good might happen, and that is why, even though there are many evils in the world, there is still a little hope." She held up a picture she had copied from a book. It was a picture of Pandora opening up the box and a whole shebang of gremlins floating out. Pandora looked extensively frightened.

On the way home, I said, "You must have been nervous."

"About what?" Phoebe said.

"About the report, Phoebe. Golly!"

"Oh no," she said. "I wasn't at all nervous."

1 **Find a quote from the story to back up each of the statements below.**

   a Mary Lou and Ben were surprised by some of the details in Phoebe's story.

   b Phoebe is nervous.

   c Ben wishes Phoebe would stop talking.

   d Ben is bothering Phoebe.

   e Mr Birkway does not quite agree about what the evils of the world are.

   f The narrator likes big words.

2 **Answer the questions below.**

   a Why is the word 'Man' capitalised?

   b Why does 'Earth' have a capital letter?

   c Why are some of Phoebe's words in *italics*?

   d What does the name 'Pandora' mean?

   e What do you think 'a whole shebang of gremlins' means?

3 **PAIR WORK. Look carefully at the lists of gifts with your partner.**

   a Look at the gifts Pandora is given. Make two lists – one of the things she is given, and one of the attributes (such as love, faith, and so on).

   b Now look at the list of things that come out of the box. Write them down. Which of the items would you classify as 'true evils' and which are things that Phoebe is scared of?

PAIR WORK. Write down, in point form, a summary of the myth of *Pandora's Box*. You will need to read the text carefully to extract the story.
Start like this:

- Zeus decided to give Man a present.
- So he …

Clauses

Clauses are groups of words with a verb. A clause is part of a sentence.

The **main** clause is the most important part of a sentence. It has the main meaning.

CONNECTIVE
/
For example: He got a present because he was lonely.

main clause   subordinate clause

The **subordinate** clause adds something extra to the main clause.

CONNECTIVE
/
For example: Pandora was curious, so she opened the box.

main clause   subordinate clause

1 **Find the main clause and the subordinate clause in each of the sentences below.**

   a Zeus gave Man a present because he was lonely.

   b After he created Pandora, he invited the gods to dinner.

   c When she received her gifts, she was grateful.

   d Because she was curious, she opened the box.

   e The evils flew out when she opened the box.

   f We can always hope because something good may happen.

2 **Give each of the main clauses below a subordinate clause. Use the connective in brackets to join the two clauses.**

   a Phoebe blushed _____. (because)

   b Ben was irritating her _____. (so)

   c Misako raised her hand _____ . (because)

   d Shigeru did not understand _____. (so)

   e Mr Birkway wanted to interrupt _____. (although)

3 **Now give each of the subordinate clauses below a main clause.**

   a _____ because he only had animals for company.

   b _____, so she would feel welcome.

   c Because of all these gifts, _____ .

   d _____, although she was forbidden to open the box.

   e _____ because she was curious.

Reading and speaking

1 **GROUP WORK. Read the text on the right. It is from the same story you have just read. Salamanca is the narrator and she is thinking about what Phoebe read to the class.**

a Make a list of five awful things in the world.

b Which things on your list can be fixed? Discuss how they can be fixed.

c Discuss how you can help someone who is going through one of the awful things on your list.

d Do you agree that people prefer to worry about things that are closer to them?

e Do you agree that most people 'seem a lot like us; sometimes cruel and sometimes kind.'?

> It seems to me that we can't explain all the truly awful things in the world like war and murder and brain tumours, and we can't fix these things, so we look at the frightening things that are closer to us and we magnify them until they burst open. Inside is something that we can manage, something that isn't as awful as it had at first seemed. It is a relief to discover that although there may be axe murderers and kidnappers in the world, most people seem a lot like us; sometimes cruel, and sometimes kind.

2 **At the end of next week, you are going to present a talk about a myth or a fable. Start doing some research now.**

- You can choose a story from anywhere in the world.
- You must introduce your story, and give its title.
- Explain why you chose that story.
- Then tell the story.
- Finally say what the moral, or message is.

Spelling and punctuation

1 **Correct the mistakes in the sentences below.**

a Now we is going to read about Anansi the spider.

b His always playing tricks on the other animals.

c Most times he gets court.

d In this next storey, Horse have a trick played on him.

e Goat sees what happens, and play a trick on Anansi.

f Their is a moral to this story.

2 Arrange the mixed up sentences below in order and punctuate them correctly.

   a animal stories many from come africa

   b moral at end the every story has a

   c prefer i the Greek myths she but likes tales fairy

   d learns a lesson anansi tricks that don't pay

   e favourite your is what story

3 Join the sentences below with a connective from the box.

> and   but   so   because   then   when   although

   a They had finished cutting the plantains. They made a fire.

   b They needed a match. Anansi sent Horse to get one.

   c Please get us some fire. We can roast the plantains.

   d Horse galloped off. Horse went to fetch some fire.

   e Horse was gone. Anansi built a fire with his own tinderbox.

Listening, reading and speaking

PAIR WORK. Many fables have animals as their main characters. Anansi, the spider, features in stories from Africa and the Caribbean. He is a trickster. Listen to the story and then read it. Answer the questions with your partner.

   a Where does the story take place?

   b Who are the main characters?

   c Write one sentence to describe what each of the main characters is like.

   d What is a plantain?

   e How do you know that the story comes from a long time ago?

   f What is the moral of the story?

Anansi and Horse

One day Anansi asked Horse to go with him to cut plantains. When they had finished cutting the plantains, they carried them out to a clearing and began to play a game – stick, lick stick. After a while Anansi said, "Brer Horse, we are hungry now but we don't have a fire to roast the plantains. Do you see that fire up there on the hill? Please gallop up there and get a lighted stick so we can make a fire and roast the plantains." Horse immediately flung up his tail and galloped off.

As soon as the horse was gone, Anansi took out a tinderbox and built a big fire. He roasted all the plantains and then he quickly ate all but four of them.

When Horse came back, Anansi explained that a man had come by, and helped him to make a fire. Anansi had roasted the plantains so that he could share them with Horse. But then another man had come by, beaten Anansi and stolen all but the four leftover plantains. Brer Horse said, "Never mind. You take two and I'll take two." And Horse took his two quite happily.

Brer Goat had been hiding behind a bush and he'd seen what Anansi had done, so the next day, he called on Anansi to go and cut plantains with him. Goat and Anansi went out, cut plantains and carried them to the clearing. Anansi then said, "Brer Goat, we are hungry now, but we don't have a fire to roast the plantains. Do you see that fire up there on the hill? Please trot up there and get a lighted stick so we can make a fire and roast the plantains." Goat trotted off, but he ran round a clump of bushes and watched Anansi.

Anansi took out his tinderbox and made a fire. Once he'd peeled all the plantains and put them on the fire to roast, Goat jumped out of the bush and grabbed a stick. He lit the stick and set fire to the grass in a circle around the fire.

"Put your hand in there and steal the plantains, Sir," he said to Anansi. Goat then jumped neatly over the ring of fire, and began to gather up the nicely roasted plantains. Anansi begged and cried for his share, but Goat took them all and ran off.

Anansi was left with absolutely none.

1 PAIR WORK. Look at the comic version below of another story about Anansi. Work out which caption on page 74 goes with which picture.

a Soon they found another nest of eggs. Firefly shone her light again, and again Anansi grabbed all the eggs.

b Anansi couldn't sleep. He was hungry. He put his hand in the pot. The lobster pinched him. "Owwww!" he cried. "A flea bit me!"

c "Let's go on an egg hunt tonight." said Firefly. "We can make egg soup for supper."

d Anansi was a clever and greedy spider.

e Anansi licked his lips. Firefly did not know that Anansi did not like to share.

f Anansi grabbed the eggs and stuffed them into his bag. Firefly was angry.

g Firefly was furious! She flew off and left Anansi alone and lost in the dark.

h One day Firefly came to visit.

i Tiger woke up. "There are no fleas in my house!" roared Tiger. He chased Anansi away, and the whole Tiger family had a good laugh – and a good bowl of egg soup!

j Anansi needed a place to sleep. He saw Tiger's house. "I have brought you some eggs," Anansi told Tiger.

k That night, firefly took Anansi to a field. She shone her light and they found some eggs in the grass.

l Tiger put the eggs in a pot. He knew Anansi was a trickster, so he hid a lobster in the pot and went to bed.

2 Now write some direct speech to fit the speech bubbles in the story. Be creative!

3 It is time to present your fable to the class. Use the score chart to do a peer assessment. Give a reason for the score you chose.

Presenting a fable

Choose 3, 2 or 1 for each criterion. 3 is best, 1 is worst.

a	good introduction	3 2 1	
b	interesting explanation of why story chosen	3 2 1	
c	exciting telling of story	3 2 1	
d	good vocabulary and grammar	3 2 1	
e	good, fluent pace	3 2 1	
f	interacted well with audience	3 2 1	
g	clear moral of the story	3 2 1	
h	good use of non-verbal communication techniques	3 2 1	

Reading and writing

In Stage 4 you learned about the structure of a good story.

Story structure

Many good stories have five stages.

climax

build-up   resolution

introduction   conclusion

1 PAIR WORK. Read the fable *Anansi and Horse* again. Does it fit the five-stage pattern? Discuss the stages of the fable with your partner.

2 Create your own fable. It can be about Anansi or you can have another animal as your main character. Use the chart on the next page to guide you in the writing process.

Step 1: Planning

Choose a setting for your fable.

Choose a hero and a villain for your fable.

Think about what might happen in your fable. Think about how your story will fit the five-stage story structure. Use the five story stages as headings. Write notes about what happens under each heading.

Think of a title for your fable.

What is the moral (lesson) of your fable?

Step 2: Writing a rough draft

Use your plan to help you write your fable in rough. Write at least one paragraph for each stage of the fable.

Step 3: Evaluating

Read your rough draft out loud to yourself and make changes if you need to.

Now read it out loud to your partner. Can they make any suggestions to improve the fable?

Write a final version of your fable, including all of the changes. Remember to write in your neatest handwriting. Add a picture that shows the characters and setting if you have time.

Thinking time

Think about how you would feel if someone cheated you like Anansi did. Present a friendship code of conduct that teaches people how to be a good friend. Tell the class about it.

7 Exploring space

1 **GROUP WORK. Read the text below about astronauts in space. Look at the pictures carefully. Then discuss the questions.**

   a What is the purpose of the text?

   b Is the style of writing personal or impersonal? Give a reason for your answer.

   c What else would be difficult to do in zero gravity?

   d What are the advantages of zero gravity?

   e Would you like to be in zero gravity? Explain why, or why not.

How do astronauts live in space?

The main difference between living in space and living on Earth is the floating problem! Here on Earth we have a force called gravity, which pulls us towards Earth, and gives us weight.

Gravity gets less and less as you move further from Earth, and if you get far enough away you become weightless and you float.

Astronauts eat food from sealed containers, and they put the empty packets into a special bin afterwards. They can't put salt and pepper on their food, because the salt and pepper floats away!

When astronauts need to sleep they tie themselves down, otherwise they could float around and bump into things. They usually sleep in sleeping bags.

Astronauts wear ordinary clothes, like tracksuits and T-shirts inside the spacecraft. They don't often wash or change their clothes. The clothes don't get dirty, and they have to save water.

Because there is no gravity, you don't use your muscles like you do on Earth. So astronauts have to exercise on special machines, to stop their muscles from wasting away.

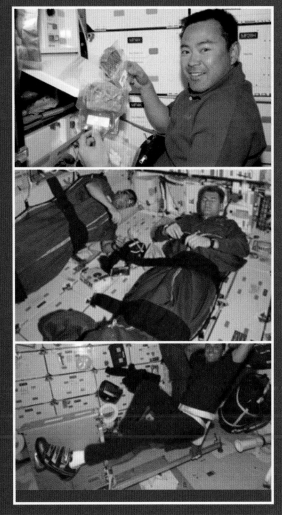

2 Imagine you are an astronaut and your bag of popcorn tears open. How would you describe the incident to:

a   your best friend back down on Earth?

b   your boss?

Think about the different language you would use.

3 GROUP WORK. Discuss how you would clean up the mess. Once you have a clever solution, elect a spokesperson to report back to the rest of the class.

Writing

Write an email to your friend explaining what happened to the popcorn.

If you have internet access in the classroom write the email for real and get your friend to reply to you.

You should write at least two paragraphs.

To:
Cc:
Subject:

Writing and speaking

1 Use computer software to create a digital presentation about space.

2 Use your digital presentation to help you give a talk to the class.

Using subordinate clauses

Complex sentences

A **complex** sentence has a main clause, and one or more subordinate clauses.

For example: The boys, **who** were all rugby players, refused to talk.

You connect the subordinate clause to the main clause with **who** or **whom** for people, and **that** or **which** for animals and things.

For example: My father hated the owl **that** hooted.

The coat, **which** I left on the chair, has disappeared.

Note that if the subordinate clause is in the middle of a sentence, it gets a comma before and after it.

1 **Find the subordinate clause in each of the sentences below and write it.**

a Astronauts, who live in space, are specially trained.

b We have a force called gravity, which pulls us to Earth.

c Jim Reilly, who is an astronaut, loves walking in space.

d "You get a great view, that you don't get from anywhere else!" he said.

e He is the reason that I want to be an astronaut.

f Chefs, who make the food on Earth, pre-package it into packets.

g They put the packets, which are empty, into a special bin.

h The clothes, which they don't wash, don't get dirty.

2 **Write your own subordinate clauses to finish the sentences below.**

a My father, _____, would never let me be an astronaut.

b The rocket, _____, was the first human-made thing in space.

c I saw the movie, _____.

d The packets, _____, go into a special bin.

e My friend, _____, is very intelligent.

Vocabulary and writing

1 Read the dictionary definition of 'Velcro' below.
Velcro was invented for space travel. It was used to
stop items from floating around the spacecraft.

> **Velcro** /'vɛlkrəʊ/ **n.** *proper.* a fastener for clothes, etc.
> consisting of two strips of nylon fabric, one looped
> and one burred, which adhere when pressed together.
> **Velcroed adj.** [F velours croché hooked velvet]

a What is the purpose of this type of writing?

b What part of speech is the word 'Velcro'?

c Why do you think it has a capital letter?

d What does 'one looped and one burred' mean?

e What is another word for 'adhere'?

f What is the adjective form of 'Velcro'?

g What language does the word come from originally?

2 There are many words
used to describe space.

a Use a thesaurus to look up
the words on the right.

b Write down at least five
synonyms for each of them.

c Write a dictionary definition for one
of the words. Use formal language
and set out the definition correctly.

d Write a paragraph about space that includes five of the synonyms.

Spelling log

Record any new words
and their synonyms in
your spelling log.

heavenly

immense

sky

void

Writing and speaking

1 PAIR WORK. Write down ten questions
you would like to ask an astronaut. Then
think up answers for your ten questions.

2 Now present your 'interview' to the class,
with one of you being a world-famous
reporter and the other an astronaut.

How to do an interview

- Plan the questions you are going
to ask, before the interview.
- Write them down.
- Use who, which, what, when,
where, why?
- Avoid 'closed' questions that
give a yes/no answer.

Listen to the text below from *A Wrinkle in Time*. Then read the text yourself.

~ A Wrinkle in Time ~

"Nnow," Mrs Which said. "Arre wee rreaddy?"

"Where are we going?" Calvin asked.

"Wwee musstt ggo bbehindd thee sshaddow."

"But we will not do it all at once," Mrs Whatsit comforted them. "We will do it in short stages." She looked at Meg. "Now we will tesser, we will wrinkle again. Do you understand?"

"No," Meg said, flatly.

Mrs Whatsit sighed. "Explanations are not easy when they are about things for which your civilisation still has no words. Calvin talked about travelling at the speed of light. You understand that, little Meg?"

"Yes," Meg nodded.

"That, of course, is the impractical, long way round. We have learned to take short cuts wherever possible."

"Sort of like in Math?"

"Like in Math." Mrs Whatsit looked over at Mrs Who. "Take your skirt and show them."

"La experiencia es la madre de la ciencia. Spanish, my dears. Cervantes. Experience is the mother of knowledge." Mrs Who took a portion of her white robe in her hands and held it tight.

"You see," Mrs Whatsit said, "if a very small insect were to move from the section of skirt in Mrs Who's right hand, to that in her left, it would be quite a long walk for him if he had to walk straight across."

Swiftly Mrs Who brought her hands, still holding the skirt, together.

"Now, you see," Mrs Whatsit said, "he would be there, without that long trip. That is how we travel."

Charles Wallace accepted this explanation serenely. Even Calvin did not seem perturbed.

"Oh dear," Meg sighed. "I guess I am a moron. I just don't get it."

"That is because you think of space only in three dimensions," Mrs Whatsit told her. "We travel in the fifth dimension. This is something you can understand Meg. Don't be afraid to try. Was your mother able to explain a tesseract to you?"

Meg sighed. "Just explain it to me."

From *A Wrinkle in Time*, by Madeleine L'Engle

Comprehension

1 **Discuss the questions below.**

a Do you understand what a 'wrinkle in time' is? Explain it to the class.

b Demonstrate how to fold time by using a piece of cloth. Show the class.

c Do you think this way of travelling will ever be possible?

d How fast would travelling like this be?

e Read the entry from the encyclopedia about the speed of light. What kind of spacecraft would we need to travel at this speed?

The speed of light

Light travels through space (and air) at a speed of 299 000 km per second (186 000 miles per second). If you could travel at that speed, you could go more than seven times round the world in a second!

Scientists believe that nothing can travel faster than light. That is because there is not enough energy in the whole universe to make even the smallest thing reach that speed.

Light takes about 8¼ minutes to reach us from the Sun. So when you see the Sun, you are seeing it as it was about 8¼ minutes ago. Reflected light takes about 1¼ seconds to reach us from the Moon.

2 **Now answer the questions below.**

a Why do you think Mrs Which sppeeeakss as she does?

b Find another word for 'tesser' in the first few paragraphs.

c What does *La experiencia es la madre de la sciencia* mean?

d How does Mrs Who demonstrate what a 'tesser' is?

e Which people understood immediately?

f Why does Meg say that she is a moron?

g In which dimension will they travel?

h Who do you think Mrs Which, Mrs Whatsit and Mrs Who are?

Punctuation and vocabulary

1 **Punctuate the sentences below correctly. Remember to use quotation marks for direct speech.**

a   charles asked what is the first dimension

b   meg replied that it was a straight line

c   he said well the second dimension would be a flat square

d   meg replied that she understood that

e   charles said and the third dimension would be a box

f   they guessed that the fourth dimension would have to do with time

g   meg asked so the fifth dimension is travelling through space and time

h   exactly said charles

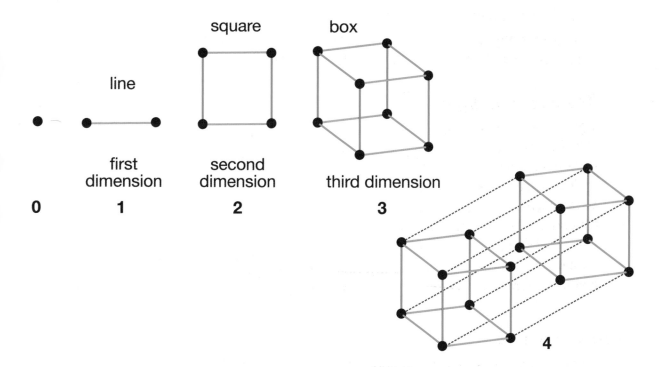

2 **You can make words into their opposites by adding the prefixes** *un–, in–* **or** *im–*. **Add a prefix to each word below to make an opposite meaning.**

possible	explored	perfect	intelligent
believable	inspired	patient	perturbed
credible	known	sane	afraid

3 **Now learn your new words for a quick spelling test.**

Reading and speaking

GROUP WORK. Read the poem below about gravity. Prepare to read it aloud for the class.

- Divide up the lines between you so everyone has some lines to say.
- Think about what actions you could do to go with your lines.
- Is there part of the poem you want to all say together?
- Do some people act while others read? You decide.

Gravity

There's something about gravity
that doesn't quite make sense to me.
I'm standing upside down, you know,
and I won't fall if I let go.
What kind of sneaky trick is that?
I bet the Earth is really flat –
but then I'd still be feet up first,
or on my head, whichever's worst.

And what if gravity let go?
What happens to me, here below?
Will I then float into the void?
Is everything we know destroyed?
Will we all head off into space,
goodbye to the whole human race?

What is this force that sucks us on,
what happens with the people gone?
Will moles get vacuumed out the ground?
Will trees uproot and spin around?
Imagine all the seas come loose,
in orbit like a watery noose
around a bare and rocky lump...
enough to make you want to jump!

I think I'll tie myself on tight
when I get into bed tonight.

Fiona Macgregor

Comprehension

Answer the questions below about the poem.

a Write down all the words that rhyme at the ends of the lines for the first verse. What kind of rhyme scheme is this?

b Write down one rhyming couplet from the poem.

c What does the word 'void' mean?

d Find an example of a simile in the third verse.

e Do you like the poem? Say why, or why not.

Figures of speech

A **metaphor** is a direct comparison between two things. For example: He is a mad dog!

A **simile** is when you compare one thing to another, using *like* or *as*.

For example: *as* big *as* a house; the Sun is *as* yellow *as* a pumpkin; he runs *like* the wind.

Writing

There are many wonderful ideas and theories about space in Unit 7. Choose the idea you like the most and write a short poem about it.

- Your poem does not have to rhyme.
- Use interesting words from your spelling log, a dictionary and a thesaurus that convey feeling and mood.
- Include similes, metaphors or personification.

Below are some examples to give you ideas.

Velcro
makes my hair
'fro
Cool space stuff
dude
I wanna have astro-
tude

Space is like a place
so big and huge
that my small brain
can't really understand it
the vast and open sky
oh wow oh why

Space is like the deepest sea
with not enough air for you and me
people in space always float around
but we like to stay on the ground

Reflection

1 **GROUP WORK. You have read three different genres in Unit 7: information text, story and poetry. Reflect on the texts and discuss the questions below.**

　a　Classify the texts as fiction or non-fiction.

　b　Explain why you do or do not like reading each genre.

2 **Look at the book covers. Which fiction genre is each book?**

a

b

c

d

3 **Make lists of what makes something an information text, a story or poetry.**

4 **Discuss the books you read at home.**

　a　Which genre do you read the most?

　b　Who is your favourite writer?

　c　Recommend your favourite writer to your group. Use language that will persuade your group members to read books by the writer.

8 Here is the news

1 **Listen to the radio news broadcast below. A news broadcast starts with the highlights or the 'breaking news'. As you listen, make a note of the main points of the news.**

Good evening. This is Dan Brown with the six o'clock news on NetWorkLive. Breaking news: An unmanned satellite has crashed into the Sahara desert, shocking local villagers in the town of Tarat. Also in the headlines: the World Environment Conference begins in Davos, raging veld fires in Cape Town, a world leader retires, a nail-biting local rescue and good news for peanut butter lovers everywhere.

But first, the big story. At five this morning a Russian satellite crashed near the town of Tarat. The huge explosion woke local villagers, many of whom thought it was a message from an angry god. "There was fire, and blinding light, and pieces of metal everywhere," one villager said. "Our whole house shook, and plates fell off the shelves," the mayor's wife complained. Russian authorities confirmed that the satellite had lost a key directional component, and plunged to earth. No one was injured in the explosion. Clean up crews will be sent to the area, although local scrap metal merchants are treating this as manna from heaven.

The World Environment Conference began in Davos yesterday, and the first item on the agenda was plastic waste. All participating countries have agreed to stop making plastic bags immediately. Plastic bottles will be phased out over a five-year period.

The veld fires in Cape Town are raging out of control, and many residents have been evacuated. An area of over 4000 hectares has burnt, and residents in the southern peninsula have been cut off from the main city of Cape Town. Firefighters are working round the clock to bring the blaze under control.

The Russian president has decided to retire and become a game farmer. He said he was finding politics, and politicians, very irritating, so he handed in his notice, and is using his retirement fund to start a game farm specialising in the rare Sabre-toothed tiger.

In local news, quick action by a beach walker saved the life of surf-skier Rob Mackenzie this morning. Mr Evan Keene, of Brown Bay, noticed a skier in trouble, and called 911. Sea Rescue was on the scene within minutes, and managed to rescue Mr Mackenzie and his ski. Mr Keene will receive an award from Sea Rescue for his assistance.

And finally, good news for peanut butter lovers everywhere. Buttercup, that world-famous brand, is introducing several new flavours – peanut and raisin, peanut and chips, and the rather interesting peanut and Kool-aid. I guess it's all a matter of taste…

That's all for now. Our next news broadcast will be at eight o'clock. Good night.

2 **Now read through the broadcast again to find the specific information below. Write down:**

a the name of the network

b the time of the news

c the name of the newsreader

d how many international stories there were

e how many local stories there were

f where the satellite fell

g what is happening in Cape Town

h who is retiring

i who or what was rescued

j why peanut butter lovers will be happy.

3 **PAIR WORK. Do you believe everything you hear on the news? Which of the stories do you think are true and which are not? Discuss this with your partner. Give reasons for your answers.**

Vocabulary

1 **The phrases below are idioms from the text you have just read.**

- Write a definition of each phrase.
- Use each phrase in a sentence of your own to show you know what it means.

a a nail-biting rescue

b manna from heaven

c phased out

d round the clock

e a matter of taste

2 **Practise saying the words in the box out loud.**

satellite	authority	peninsula
environment	immediately	retirement
conference	component	assistance
everywhere	several	
explosion	participation	

- Find the parts of the words that are tricky to spell.
- Write the words and circle the silent vowels.
- Finally, learn the words for a spelling test.

Reading

Read the eyewitness account on the next page. As you read, think about the following questions.

a Why is it called an 'eyewitness' account?

b How is the language in the account different from the language in the news broadcast?

> **Recounts**
>
> Non-fiction recounts usually include:
> - names of people, places and things.
> - the past tense.
> - paragraphs.
> - action verbs.
> - quotations.
> - time connectives.

Register

People speak and write differently depending on where they are and who they are with. For example, you would speak very differently to your head teacher than you would to your best friend.

To head teacher: Sir, we appreciate you coming to watch our class play.

To friend: What's up? It's awesome that you came to watch our class play.

Eyewitness account: Sea Rescue

It was early on Saturday morning, the tenth of March, I think it was, and I was walking on the beach when I saw a guy dragging his surf-ski into the water. I noticed that he wasn't wearing a life jacket but he seemed to be quite fit so I stopped and watched him as he set off into the waves.

The sea was really rough and he took quite a pounding trying to get through the waves. Then a huge wave came through and I got quite worried. The wave smashed over him and for a while I couldn't see him. Then his surf-ski popped out the water but he was nowhere in sight. I immediately dialled 911 and gave directions for help – "Brown Bay Beach, surf-skier in trouble, hurry!"

His head appeared above the water and he waved his arm in distress – I waved back and then he got pulled under again. When his head appeared again I yelled that the Sea Rescue was on its way – I don't know if he heard me but the rescue boat was there within minutes.

They approached from behind the breakers and while two men grabbed the surf-ski, another two threw out a life ring on a rope, which the surf-skier managed to catch. It was all over within half an hour. A very professional bunch I must say. Although the skier was a bit stupid to go out in those conditions without a life jacket in my opinion. But all's well that ends well, as they say.

Advice from the surf-skier

1. Should you go paddling in the ocean, always wear a life jacket.
2. Never go paddling in bad conditions as you could drown.
3. I would always wear a leash if I were you, so you are tied to your ski.
4. You should be grateful for the kindness of strangers.

Comprehension

**PAIR WORK. Discuss the questions below.
Then write the answers.**

a Is the account written in the first person or the third person?

b Write down a sentence from the text to support your answer.

c Write down one phrase that is slang or informal language.

d What does 'took quite a pounding' mean?

e Give an alternative word for 'bunch'.

f What is a 'leash'?

g Write out the following sentence in more formal language: I saw a guy dragging his surf-ski.

h Say what 'All's well that ends well' means, in your own words.

i Find a fact in the account.

j Find an opinion in the account.

Point of view

The point of view is the angle from which the story is told.

- First person: told by someone who is part of the action and uses the pronouns *I*, *me* and *we*.

- Third person: told by someone who sees all the action and uses the pronouns *he*, *she*, *it*, *they*, *his*, *hers*, *its* and *theirs*.

Using modal verbs

Read the information about modal verbs.

❶ **Find three modals in the surf-skier's advice.**

❷ **Use the modals in sentences of your own.**

❸ **Fill each gap in the paragraph below with a different modal verb.**
I think that Mr Keene _____ receive an award from Sea Rescue. _____ he do so, I will be the first to congratulate him. I _____ be very proud of him.

Modal verbs

We use the modal verbs **should**, **would** and **could** to talk about possible events or situations.

*If anyone **should** ask for me, I'll be paddling in my surf-ski.*

***Should** you arrive late, you will not be allowed to compete.*

*I **would** hate to be lost at sea.*

*If we were wealthy, we **would** travel more.*

*It **could** rain on Saturday.*

*He **could** have drowned.*

Write a report about the sea rescue. Your report should be in the past tense as you are reporting on something that has already happened. Use the following chart to guide you in the writing process.

Step 1: Planning

Skim through the news broadcast and the eyewitness account and write notes about the sea rescue. Answer the following questions.
- Who was involved?
- What happened?
- When did it happen?
- Where did it happen?
- Why did it happen?

Talk to your partner.
- Compare the notes you have made.
- Add missing information to your notes.

Write a heading for your report.
- Is it interesting?
- Will it capture the reader's interest?

Think about the style and tone of your report. Write notes to help you remember your ideas.
- Use formal words.
- Do not use slang.
- Be brief.

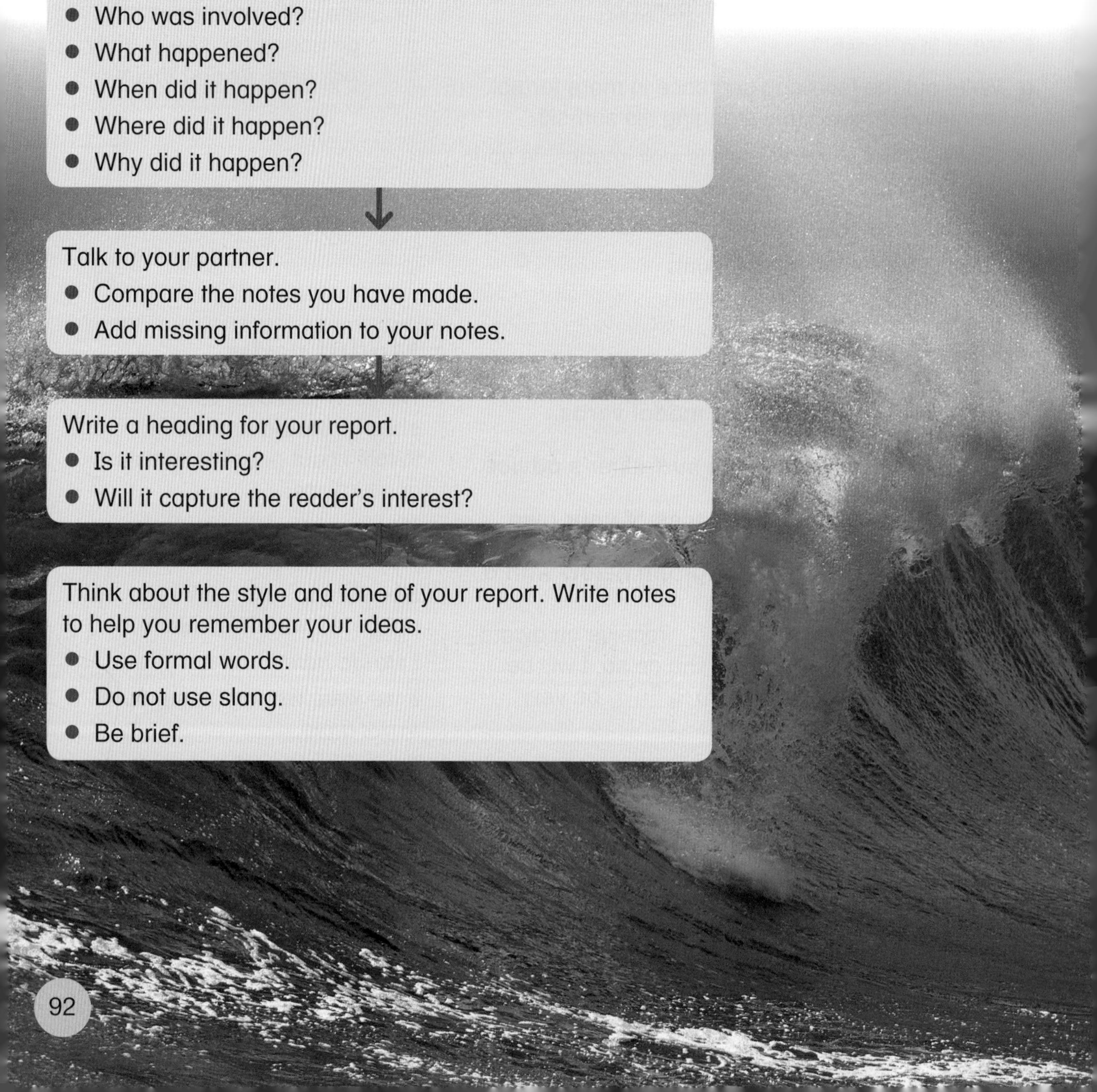

Step 2: Writing a rough draft

Use your notes to help you write a rough draft of your report.
- Write an opening sentence that sets the scene and makes someone want to read on.
- Organise your report into short paragraphs. Decide on main and supporting ideas for each paragraph.
- Include a quotation.
- Include all details.
- Consider your choice of words.
- Construct sentences properly.
- Use punctuation correctly.

Step 3: Evaluating

Read your rough draft out loud to yourself. Think about whether your words help the reader to clearly imagine what you are writing about. Make changes if you need to.

Now read the report out loud to your partner. Can they follow the report? Can they make any suggestions to improve it?

Write a final version of your report, including all of the changes.

Step 4: Performance and reflection

Read your report to your group. Use appropriate tone and volume.

Discuss the reports after each presentation.
- Are all details included?
- Is the report easy to follow?
- Is the style of the report formal and brief?

Using apostrophes

1. Find all the contractions in the eyewitness account on page 90 and write them out in full.

2. Rewrite the paragraph below, replacing the words in bold with contractions.

> I **did not** have my life jacket with me. It **does not** matter how good a swimmer you are, if you get into trouble, you need a life jacket. **I am** very lucky that Mr Mackenzie saw me. I **could have** been in big trouble. **He is** a hero. **I cannot** thank him enough. **That is** all I have to say.

Apostrophes

The **apostrophe** (') is used to replace a letter that gets left out. This is called a contraction. You often find contractions in informal writing or when the writer is writing dialogue and wants to show what real speech sounds like.

For example: "I'll put on the radio," instead of "I will put on the radio".

Common phrases that have apostrophes are:

I will – I'll	I will not – I won't
do not – don't	I cannot – I can't
he is – he's	I am – I'm
they are – they're	it is – it's
that is – that's	what is – what's

Reading and speaking

PAIR WORK. Read the poem on the right about the apostrophe. First read it silently and then read it out loud to your partner.

Comprehension

PAIR WORK. Discuss the questions below. Then write your answers.

a Where would you put an apostrophe in the first line of the poem?

b What language feature is 'hovering like a paper kite'?

c Where would the apostrophe go in line 7?

d Find a metaphor you like in the poem. Say what is being compared to what.

e What kind of character does the poet give to the apostrophe? Give **one** phrase from the poem that supports your answer.

f How do you think the poet would feel about having his poem used in an activity like this?

Apostrophe

twould be nice to be
an apostrophe
floating
above an s
hovering
like a paper kite
in between the its
eavesdropping, tiptoeing
high above the thats
an inky comet
spiralling
the highest tossed
of hats

Roger McGough

Using punctuation

1 **Use an apostrophe to show possession.**

    a the shoes of Roger   <u>Roger's shoes</u>

    b the letters of my mother

    c the friend of Lily

    d the dress of the bride

    e the voice of the newsreader

    f the friend of Ross

    g the board of the surfer

    h the uniforms of the girls

    i the news of her grandmother

    j the march of the women

> ### Apostrophes ('s)
>
> **The apostrophe 's** shows the possessive form of the noun.
>
> For example:
>
> The pot of the cook – the cook*'s* pot.
>
> The friend of Zac – Zac*'s* friend.
>
> If the noun ends on an *–s*, then put the apostrophe after the *s*.
>
> For example:
>
> The books of the girls – the girl*s'* books.
>
> The hat of James – Jame*s'* hat.

2 **Punctuate the sentences below correctly.**

    a the headlines said quick action saves a skiers life

    b i dont believe the news about different peanut butter flavours

    c my mothers friend knows the man who almost drowned

    d the newsreader said its all a matter of taste

    e my fathers cousins live in cape town near the fires

    f whos coming with us on the womens march

    g my sisters landlady thinks hes quite helpful

    h shes always cutting out photos of celebrities from the papers

3 **Correct the errors in the sentences below.**

    a They're are far more strange things their than you can possibly imagine!

    b Whose the person you were talking too?

    c We looked threw her photographs of the fires, than we went to lunch.

    d You're brother works oversees, does'nt he?

    e Their waiting at the stationary shop for their order to go threw.

1 GROUP WORK. Read the article below. Then discuss the questions.

a In what sort of magazine would you find an article like this?

b How would you describe the kind of language used? Look at words as well as the kinds of sentences in the article.

c Make a list of all the informal expressions in the article.

d Find the contractions and decide what letters the apostrophe is replacing.

Media reports

Media reports, such as magazine articles, are usually interesting and informative to keep the reader's interest. They may have:

- powerful, eye-catching titles.
- columns.
- paragraphs.

Can fame make the world a better place?

The organisation DoSomething.org has released its 7th annual 'Celebs Gone Good' list. The list ranks the top 20 celebs who use their fame (and fortune) to help others. For the third time in a row, singer Taylor Swift scoops the number one slot. Successful, smart and generous? That's the kind of girl we like!

Taylor Swift donated all of the money she earned from the sale of her single *Welcome to New York* to New York City Public Schools. So, if you bought this song, give yourself a high-five – because you've also done some good.

The actress Laverne Cox came in at number two. This ultracool feminist icon helped to get people talking about tolerating difference this year. Beyoncé slotted in 3rd for her #BeyGood campaign. Miley Cyrus follows closely behind for her work around the serious issue of youth homelessness. And rounding out the top 5 is yet another female star,

Emma Watson, who blew the world away with a hard-hitting speech on gender equality at the UN. She also set up the #HeForShe campaign.

So … this year, it's all about girl power! Go girls – you rock.

2 Rewrite the article about celebrities and their charitable causes for a formal newspaper. Below are some guidelines.

- make sure you use complete sentences
- avoid using contractions
- avoid informal language or slang
- avoid giving your own opinion in the article – just provide your readers with facts

Listening and writing

1 Watch the news on television tonight. Your teacher will give you a form like the one on the right to fill in.

2 Compare your completed forms in class. Get into groups according to who watched the same news programme on the same channel.

- Go through your forms together.
- Add any information you may have missed.
- Correct any mistakes you may have made.

Time	
Channel	
Reporter	
Headlines	
Main stories	
International	
Local	
Funny story	
Sports results	
Weather	

Listening and speaking

1 PAIR WORK. Produce a news broadcast for the class. Follow the structure of the news broadcast on page 87. You should have at least three main stories in your broadcast and one funny or local story.

2 Present your news broadcast to the class.

Thinking time

How might the following people react when they read the eye-witness account?

- the mother of the surf-skier
- the surf-skier
- the eye-witness
- the Sea Rescue team

9 Our changing Earth

GROUP WORK. Read the text *Africa* and discuss the questions below.

a What is the purpose of the text *Africa*?

b What genre is *Africa*? How do you know?

c Which words convey feeling and mood?

d Do you think the commentary is sequenced well? Why?

e Which changes would you make to the sequence? Why?

Commentaries

Commentaries are non-fiction texts. They:
- are persuasive.
- are informative.
- contain personal opinions.
- demonstrate a consistent viewpoint.

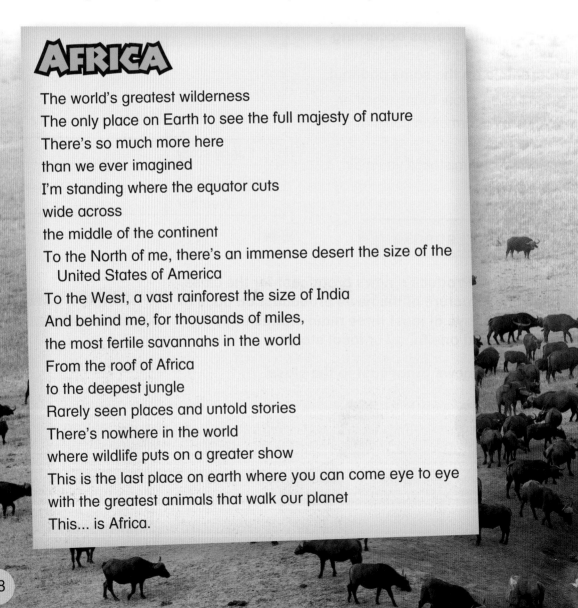

AFRICA

The world's greatest wilderness

The only place on Earth to see the full majesty of nature

There's so much more here

than we ever imagined

I'm standing where the equator cuts

wide across

the middle of the continent

To the North of me, there's an immense desert the size of the
    United States of America

To the West, a vast rainforest the size of India

And behind me, for thousands of miles,

the most fertile savannahs in the world

From the roof of Africa

to the deepest jungle

Rarely seen places and untold stories

There's nowhere in the world

where wildlife puts on a greater show

This is the last place on earth where you can come eye to eye

with the greatest animals that walk our planet

This... is Africa.

Vocabulary

Answer the questions below. Write your answers.

a   How many synonyms for 'big' can you find in the text? Use each synonym in a sentence.

b   Write the root word for each of the following words: 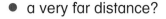 wilderness   greatest   untold

c   Break the following words into syllables: majesty   equator   immense

d   If the words 'greatest' and 'deepest' describe the wilderness and the jungle, what words would you use for:

- a very big mountain?
- a very small hummingbird?
- a very far distance?
- a very beautiful scene?

e   What do you think a 'savannah' is?

f   Find a synonym for 'forest'.

g   What is the opposite of 'rarely'?

h   What does the expression 'eye to eye' mean?

i   Find and write out two contractions in the text.

j   What is the meaning of 'roof' and 'show' in the commentary? Use the words in sentences that show a different meaning.

Writing and speaking

Remember!
Use words that convey feeling and mood.

1 Write a commentary that will introduce a TV documentary about your country or your continent. You can follow the style of David Attenborough's commentary used in *Africa* or develop your own style.

- Evaluate your writing using the checklist on page 9.
- PAIR WORK. Swap your introduction with your partner and correct each other's work.

2 Read your commentary to the class. Use as much expression as you can to convey your meaning.

Reading aloud

- Vary your **pace**. Read slowly to build suspense or quickly when there is a lot of action.
- Change your **intonation** – the pitch of your voice; speak higher when you are excited and lower when the action is slow or you want to build suspense.
- Remember the audience – make eye contact when there's a pause, **project** your voice so that everyone can hear you, and use gestures to make the reading interesting.

---

3 Watch a trailer for the BBC video of David Attenborough's *Africa* online. Discuss the following questions in class.

a Do you like how he introduced the video?

b Was it as you imagined, from reading the text?

c What do you think of his commentary?

d How does the soundtrack add meaning to the images?

GROUP WORK. Read the following short biography about Sir David Attenborough. Then discuss the questions below the text.

Sir David Attenborough is one of the most widely respected TV broadcasters. He is famous as the face and the 'voice' of natural history documentaries.

David was brought up in Leicester and went to Clare College, Cambridge, to study Natural Sciences. He graduated in 1947, and then spent two years in the navy.

When he left the navy, he worked as an editor of children's books.

In 1950 he applied to the BBC for a job. He was rejected at first, but then he got onto a three-month training programme, and did very well as a fledgling TV broadcaster. Many years later, he was put in charge of all non-fiction broadcasts, and eventually the BBC's many natural history programmes.

From 1965 to 1969 Attenborough was controller of BBC2 where he made sure there was a wide variety of interesting programmes for viewers.

However, most people remember David Attenborough for the natural history series that he wrote and produced. These combine excellent photography and his famous voiceover commentary, and appeal to young and old alike.

a What information do you expect to find in a biography?

b What information is missing from the biography?

c What sources could you use to find the missing information?

d Do you think the biography is sequenced well? Give a reason for your answer.

e Which changes would you make to the sequence? Explain why.

Research a famous person and write an informative biography. Use the planning frame below to guide you through the writing process.

1 PLAN

a Decide who you are going to write about.

b Do research to find out about the person.

- Use books or the internet.
- Make careful notes from your research.

2 WRITE

Use your plan to help you write a rough draft.

- Consider the purpose.
- Decide on main and supporting ideas for each paragraph.
- Use appropriate content and language.
- Write clearly and fluently.

BIOGRAPHY

3 EVALUATE

Read your rough draft and consider the following:

- Is it informative and easy to read?
- Do your sentences make sense?
- Have you used punctuation correctly?
- Are words spelled correctly? Use a dictionary or spell check to check the spelling of words you are unsure about.

4 REVISE

a Make corrections.

b Give your biography to your partner to read. Ask them to comment on it and suggest improvements.

c Make the changes that your partner suggests. Then read your work and edit it carefully one last time

d Present a final version, including all changes.

Read the information text below and look at the pictures.

The Greenhouse Effect

The world is warming up a little more every year, and the warmer it gets, the more **unpredictable** the weather will be. So, why is this happening?

Scientists think they know why. When we burn fuel – like oil, or coal, or wood – we make a gas called **carbon dioxide** (CO_2). Today there is more CO_2 in the air than there has been for more than half a million years. Together with other gases, carbon dioxide acts like a greenhouse, trapping the heat from the Sun's rays in the **atmosphere**. Think of what would happen if you sat outside on a sunny day in a plastic raincoat. You'd get hotter and hotter.

Trees use up carbon dioxide in the air. If we cut down forests, we have fewer trees to help control carbon dioxide. Also, cities are growing and there are more and more cars and factories, which all pump out carbon dioxide into the air. So the problem of too much carbon dioxide in the air gets worse.

The seas are warming up too, and the massive **ice sheets** at the North Pole and the **South Pole** have started to melt. If the ice sheets melt, this will unlock a huge amount of water.

Sea levels all around the world will rise and this means there will be more floods.

These changes lead to natural disasters, like **drought** in some areas, and floods in others. Changing weather patterns also mean more hurricanes and typhoons. Often, these natural disasters affect children. Later in this unit, you will read more about children who are learning to live with climate change, and who are thinking about ways to get ready for the future.

Vocabulary

1 The printers have mixed up the glossary for *The Greenhouse Effect* text. Match the correct word to its definition.

2 Use each word in a sentence.

Spelling log

Record interesting words from the article in your spelling log.

Glossary

1 atmosphere
2 carbon dioxide
3 droughts
4 ice sheets
5 South Pole
6 sea levels
7 unpredictable

a a gas that is produced by burning fuels

b not able to be predicted; not able to be known beforehand

c a layer of air around the earth

d no rain for a very long time

e the point furthest south on Earth

f the height of the sea's surface

g layers of ice that cover large areas of land for a long period of time

Comprehension

1 Choose the correct ending for each sentence.

a The climate
- is becoming more unpredictable.
- is getting colder.

b In some places it's getting drier, and in others
- it's getting wetter.
- hurricanes are coming.

c The greenhouse effect is caused by
- less carbon dioxide in the air than before.
- more carbon dioxide in the air than before.

d Carbon dioxide is
- given off by trees.
- taken in by trees.

e If ice sheets melt
- the South Pole will melt.
- sea levels will rise.

2 PAIR WORK. Draw a scientific diagram to show how the greenhouse effect works. Label your diagram with the following labels: carbon dioxide, heat trapped, atmosphere, Sun's rays. Give your diagram a title.

3 Make a list of the things that change because of the world getting warmer each year. Compare your list with your partner's. Add anything you may have left out.

PAIR WORK. Remind yourself of the features of information texts on page 40. Read the texts and then discuss the questions.

A hurricane is a huge tropical storm. It's hundreds of kilometres wide and spins round in a circle. In the middle, the 'eye' of the storm is calm. Hurricanes are given names like Katrina, Ike or Noel. Hurricanes need warm sea water to develop and grow. They do terrible damage when they reach land, but at that point, they begin to get weaker and fade away.

a hurricane

wall of cloud and storm developing

eye

warm sea

The spinning wall of cloud and storm is where the wind speed is highest and rainfall heaviest.

HURRICANE ALERT ● How to be prepared!

Follow these steps, so you will always be prepared for a hurricane alert.

- ✔ First, buy a waterproof container, and keep it in a place that is safe, and easy to get to. This is your 'hurricane corner'.
- ✔ Put all your important papers, like your passport, in this container.
- ✔ Keep emergency cash in the container too.
- ✔ Add supplies like a torch, matches, candles and other useful items.
- ✔ In the same area, keep a change of clothing in a plastic bag, and spare toiletries, like a toothbrush.
- ✔ Finally add some bottled water to your hurricane corner.
- ✔ Make a family plan about what to do and where to go if there is a hurricane alert.

a What is the purpose of each text?

b Are the texts written in an impersonal or personal style?

c Are the texts fiction or non-fiction? How do you know?

d Which features make the texts easy to read?

e What is a 'hurricane corner'?

f Tell your partner what the hurricane diagrams explain.

Using comparative words

Complete the sentences below with the correct form of the words in brackets.

a The wind speed is at its _____ (high) and the rainfall is at
its _____ (heavy) in the spinning wall of cloud and storm.

b Hurricanes begin to get _____ (weak) as they reach land.

c The eye is the _____ (calm) part of the hurricane.

d Hurricanes can bring gigantic storm waves of _____ (most) than
seven metres high.

e Hurricanes used to happen _____ (least)
often in the past.

Reading

**You are going to read three diary
entries together as a class in
preparation for a group project this
week. As you read think about:**

- what the three diary entries have in common.
- what plans the writers are making for when
  they are older.

a Read Shumi's diary entry. She lives
in Bangladesh.

Shumi and her
little brother
outside her
house.

The roads are higher than the
fields, so we can move about
easily. But in the floods, water
covers the roads, and we
can't find our way.

I'm Shumi and I live in Bangladesh.
When the floods came last year
I picked up my little brother and
ran to the road, which is on high
ground. The water crept higher
and higher until it reached my
knees. I was so scared, but my
dad came and carried us into
the house. We climbed up to the
roof and stayed there for five
days. There was no fresh water
to drink and afterwards I had a
bad fever.

When I get older I'll tie ropes
along the roads, so that people
can see them even in a flood and
they won't drown.

b Kathure lives in Kenya, Africa, where there has been a bad drought for many years. Read her diary entry.

I'm Kathure. I don't understand climate change, but I know that the rivers have dried up and I have to walk a long way to collect water. I only have one meal a day, which I'm given at school. I feel so bad when I see my baby brother crying because he's hungry, and I can't do anything. I wish I could change this.

When I grow up, I will plant crops that don't need much rain to grow. Then my family will have food.

Joy is Kathure's cousin. She is grinding millet to make flour. Millet doesn't need so much water to grow.

Here is Kathure with her mother, granny and little brother. Kathure walks five kilometres to collect water before she goes to school.

c Now read about Jude, who lives in Haiti, in the Caribbean.

This is Jude.

My name is Jude and I live on the coast in Haiti. One night Hurricane Ike came. Dad had boarded up the house, but he's a policeman and was at work. Outside, the road turned into a river rushing past. It was full of all kinds of stuff – dead chickens and goats and lumps of wood smashing into everything. Then it went dark. The power was off and water was pouring into the house. Mum grabbed me and my little brother and held us tight. I was very scared. Scared to die, scared that the water would take away my family and my friends and also afraid to lose my house because we didn't have enough money to build another one.

Our house survived, but in the morning I saw my friend's roof was torn off, power lines were ripped up, and buildings were smashed. Many people died that night.

When I grow up, I'll make houses that don't break up when hurricanes come.

Flooding in Jacmel, Haiti, after Hurricane Ike

GROUP RESEARCH PROJECT

1 **GROUP WORK. Research a natural disaster. Your group will be required to:**

   a present a short news broadcast about the disaster.

   b write a diary entry of someone who was affected by the disaster.

   c write a poem about the disaster.

   d present a practical step-by-step plan of what you as a group could do to help.

2 **Make a poster about your research project. At the end of the week you will be required to read the news and present and talk about your poster.**

You need to decide:

- who will write which piece of text.
- who will read the news.
- who will present the poster, read the poem and discuss the plan.

Make sure everyone in the group has a role to play and share the work out equally. Each group member should be doing some writing and some speaking.

Thinking time

Talk about how readers might react differently to the same text depending on where they are reading it. Give reasons for your answers.

a How do you think people from Africa will react when they read about:
- the beauty of Africa on page 98?
- the drought in Kenya, Africa on page 107?

b How do you think someone who doesn't live in Africa will react when they read the texts?

Text acknowledgements

The publishers gratefully acknowledge the permissions granted to reproduce copyright material in the book. Every effort has been made to contact the holders of copyright material, but if any have been inadvertently overlooked, the Publisher will be pleased to make the necessary arrangements at the first opportunity.

Cover illustration: *Alice in Wonderland* Reprinted by permission of HarperCollins*Publishers* Ltd © 2015 Emma Chichester Clark.

Alice in Wonderland Reprinted by permission of HarperCollins*Publishers* Ltd © 2015 Emma Chichester Clark; *The Secret Garden* Reprinted by permission of HarperCollins*Publishers* Ltd © 2016 Fleur Hitchcock, illustrated by Laszlo Veres; *Twinkle, Twinkle, Firefly* Reprinted by permission of HarperCollins*Publishers* Ltd © 2010 John Agard and Grace Nichols, illustrated by Satoshi Kitamura; *Two Animal Tales from Africa* Reprinted by permission of HarperCollins*Publishers* Ltd © 2017 Beverley Birch, illustrated by Daniele Fabbri; *Living with Climate Change* Reprinted by permission of HarperCollins*Publishers* Ltd © 2009 Alison Sage.

We are grateful to the following for permission to reproduce copyright material:
Extracts on pp.1–3 from *Saffy's Angel* by Hilary McKay, first published by Hodder Children's Books in 2001, new edition 2021 by Macmillan Children's Books, an imprint of Pan Macmillan, copyright © Hilary McKay, 2001. Reproduced with the permission of Macmillan Publishers International Ltd; Margaret K. McElderry Books, an imprint of Simon & Schuster Children's Publishing Division; and The Bent Agency on behalf of the author. All rights reserved; Extracts on pp.7, 66–67, 70 from *Walk Two Moons* by Sharon Creech, first published by Macmillan Children's Books, an imprint of Pan Macmillan, 1994, copyright © Sharon Creech, 1994, Reproduced by permission of Macmillan Publishers International Limited and HarperCollins*Publishers*; Extracts on p.10 from *The Guinness Book of Names, 7th Revised Edition* by Leslie Dunkling, published by Guinness World Records Limited; Extracts on pp.20–22, 27 from *Wayside School is Falling Down* by Louis Sachar, illustrated by Adam McCauley, pp.1–7, 143, text copyright © Louis Sachar, 1989. Reproduced by permission of Bloomsbury Publishing Plc; and HarperCollinsPublishers; The poem on p.28 "When the Teacher Isn't Looking" by Kenn Nesbitt, published in *When The Teacher isn't Looking: And Other Funny School Poems* by Kenn Nesbitt, Meadowbrook Press, copyright © 2005. Reproduced by permission of Running Press Kids, an imprint of Hachette Book Group, Inc.; An extract on p.40 adapted from *Rainbow Reading Level 5 – Move Your Body: Body Art* by Cheryl Minkley, copyright © Cambridge University Press, 2009. Reproduced with permission of the Licensor through PLSclear; Extracts and image on pp.55–56, 62–63 from *The Whale Rider* by Witi Ihimaera, Penguin, New Zealand, 2008, copyright © Witi Ihimaera. Reproduced with permission from Penguin Random House New Zealand; The poem on p.64 'Sea Fever' by John Masefield. Reproduced with permission from The Society of Authors as the literary Representatives of the Estate of John Masefield; Extracts on p.72 from 'Anansi and Horse' by Alexander Archibald, published in *Jamaica Anansi Stories* by Martha Warren Beckwith, 1924, used under the Creative Commons Attribution-ShareAlike License. Adapted by Karen Morrison in *Caribbean Comprehension: An integrated, skills based approach Book 5*, copyright © Hodder Education, 2014. Reproduced by permission of Hodder Education; Extracts on pp.73–74 from "Anansi and Firefly go Hunting" from *Rainbow Reading Level 4 – Life and Living: Anansi and the Firefly* by Emma Attwell, copyright © Cambridge University Press, 2009. Reproduced with permission of the Licensor through PLSclear; Extract on p.77 from *Rainbow Reading Level 5 – Space Workers* by Daphne Paizee, copyright © Cambridge University Press, 2009. Reproduced with permission of the Licensor through PLSclear; Dictionary definition on p.80, 'velcro' from *The Oxford American Minidictionary*, copyright © Oxford University Press, Inc, 2004. Reproduced with permission of the Licensor through PLSclear; Extract on pp.81–82 from *A Wrinkle in Time* by Madeleine L'Engle, Penguin Books. Reproduced by permission of Aaron M. Priest Literary Agency; The poem on p.94 'Apostrophe' from *All the Best: The Selected Poems of Roger McGough* by Roger McGough. Reprinted by permission of Peters Fraser & Dunlop (www.petersfraserdunlop.com) on behalf of Roger McGough; and an extract on p.98 from David Attenborough's Africa (BBC) – Introduction, copyright © BBC Worldwide; Biography on p.101, Sir David Attenborough, adapted from http://www.biographyonline.net/scientists/david-attenborough.html, with permission from Tejvan Pettinger.

In some instances we have been unable to trace the owners of copyright material, and we would appreciate any information that would enable us to do so.

Photo acknowledgements

The publishers wish to thank the following for permission to reproduce photographs. Every effort has been made to trace copyright holders and to obtain their permission for the use of copyright materials. The publishers will gladly receive any information enabling them to rectify any error or omission at the first opportunity.

(t = top, c = centre, b = bottom, r = right, l = left)

p8 Monkey Business Images/Shutterstock, p11 sunabesyou/Shutterstock, p12 Rich Carey/Shutterstock, p14 amiminkz/Shutterstock, p14bl NAS CREATIVES/Shutterstock, p15tl sakepaint/Shutterstock, p15tr monika3steps/Shutterstock, p15bl stockcreations/Shutterstock, p15br andras_csontos/Shutterstock, p16t otnaydur/Shutterstock, p16b Charlie Edward/Shutterstock, p17tcl michaeljung/Shutterstock, p17tl Liquorice Legs/Shutterstock, p17tcc Syda Productions/Shutterstock, p17tc Pressmaster/Shutterstock, p17tr bikeriderlondon/Shutterstock, p17bcl Shenjun Zhang/Shutterstock, p17bcc Rob Marmion/Shutterstock, p17bl hxdbzxy/Shutterstock, p17bc Tyler Olson/Shutterstock, p17br Charlie Edward/Shutterstock, p19 Tyler Olson/Shutterstock, p20 Lorelyn Medina/Shutterstock, p28 James Francis/Shutterstock, p40tr Blend Images/Shutterstock, p40bl Delpixel/Shutterstock, p40br Nadezhda Bolotina/Shutterstock, p41c Penguin Random House, p41r © British Library Board, All Rights Reserved/Bridgeman Images, p43 Everett Historical Shutterstock, p50 © British Library Board. All Rights Reserved/Bridgeman Images, p51tcl Valua Vitaly/Shutterstock, p51tcl Lopolo/Shutterstock, p51bcl Arvind Balaraman Shutterstock, p51bc Serhiy Kobyakov/Shutterstock, p54 Sujono sujono/Shutterstock, p59 Arnoud Quanjer/Shutterstock, p64 Kostyantyn Ivanyshen/Shutterstock, p65l Fotoluminate LLC/Shutterstock, p65cl fluke samed/Shutterstock, p65cr lapas77/Shutterstock, p65r wavebreakmedia/Shutterstock, p68 Encyclopaedia Britannica/UIG/Getty Images, p77t, c ,b NASA, p79 NASA, p87 TZIDO SUN/Shutterstock, p88 michaeljung/Shutterstock, p89 xenia_ok/Shutterstock, p90t waniuszka/Shutterstock, p90b Dan Thornberg/Shutterstock, p92 irabel8/Shutterstock, p96 Image Press Agency/Alamy Stock Photo, p98–99 Andrzej Kubik/Shutterstock, p100 Jason Maehl/Shutterstock, p101 Stuart C. Wilson/Getty Images, p102 ajt/Shutterstock, p103 Lára órðardóttir/The Shoot Nations Project, p106bl GMB Akash, p106tr GMB Akash, p107tr Rebecca Nduku, p107c Rebecca Nduku, p107l Rafaelle Castera, p107br Plan.